Go Away Come Closer

Go Away Come Closer

When What You Need the Most is What You Fear the Most

A Book About Intimacy

Terry Hershey

WORD PUBLISHING
Dallas · London · Vancouver · Melbourne

GO AWAY, COME CLOSER

The poem "God's Fool," by Lois Cheney is quoted from *God Is No Fool,* reproduced by permission of Abingdon Press, Nashville, Tennessee.

Library of Congress Cataloging-in-Publication Data

Hershey, Terry.
Go away, come closer : when what you need the most is what you fear the most / Terry Hershey
p. cm.
Includes bibliographical references.
ISBN 0-8499-0771-3
1. Intimacy. I. Title.
BF575.I5H47 1990
158'.2—dc20 89-70753
CIP

Printed in the United States of America

12349 AGF 98765432

To
Norva

Acknowledgments

This book is a collection of reflections from my own journey toward intimate relationships. It is a journey full of surprises, unseen pitfalls, unexpected joys—and is never easily reduced to a formula. Which is why the hoped for comfort that would come from isolation and easy answers is out of the question, and the ongoing input, dialogue and requisite friction that comes from being with friends is essential.

Much of this book is drawn from that input, dialogue and friction, and I owe a debt to those who through their persistence, commitment and respect have contributed to the wealth of resources which sustain me on my journey. Thanks to my covenant group for their support. To my friend Rich Hurst, for his unflagging encouragement. To my pastor, Ben Patterson, for his ongoing affirmation. To my publisher Word, and especially to Joey Paul, for his belief in the book and the message it contains. And to my wife, Norva, for her commitment to be a loving partner in a world which finds such devotion passé.

Contents

"The glory of God is man fully alive."

Irenaeus

Preface

Intimacy is not easy to understand—or to achieve for that matter. And the word "achieve" betrays our need to reduce intimacy to some pragmatic possession, to that which can be purchased, or acquired by means of invoking the correct formula from the pages of the newest bestseller on relationships. We'll get it right and learn the answer some day, we optimistically tell ourselves.

At the same time, we bring to this discussion the pulse of several conflicting messages about our identity, love, romance, sex, self-worth, fidelity, commitment, family, and neediness. Some are cultural, some religious, some personal. But each is strong, and in some way, each continues to shape the way we deal with our relationships. Although the temptation to bury is strong, we need the permission to face these messages head on.

There are some times, however, when we wonder if we're

not simply playing out a predetermined script. And sometimes we wonder if there's any script at all. We might feel like Keith Miller when he says that, "It was as if other people had been given a secret manual about how to get along and be loved and at home in life—and I hadn't got one" (Miller, *Sin,* p. 4).

Intimacy is a subject mired in the clay of cultural misconception, personal fear, and the memories of soured good intentions and broken hearts—memories sometimes real, sometimes imagined. Many among us have surrendered to the fate of second best (wondering if maybe that's not the best we can hope for in this world of hedging our bets), or have latched on to a relationship scenario that, like a merry-go-round, takes us nowhere and plays the same old tune (and yet, we say, not quite convinced, "It's better than nothing . . . isn't it?"). And many have confined themselves to a prison of self-doubt (even self-hate), or—even more confining—to the prison of continued and relentless introspection (fueled by too many self-help books?). This leads some to the point of cynicism or even despair. Still others have sought the assistance of a guru to lead them to enlightenment, or have built a fortress of protection only to find themselves angry that no one dares to see if anyone is home. And still others continually return to the scene of some relational crime from the past, replaying the grievance on their memory video, hoping against hope for a new ending.

We are a wounded generation. And nowhere is this more apparent than in the areas of intimacy and relationships.

I wonder . . .

Why do we say we want relationships, but wonder whether they are worth the effort?

Why do we invite others into our lives, only to smother them, or wonder why we see them as intruders?

Why do we espouse direct and open communication, but wonder why we opt for mixed messages and innuendo—and then chide ourselves for such behavior?

Why do we yearn for family, when our own family system

is laced with repressed emotion, passive aggression, and conditional love?

Why do we want someone to care—to really care—but then find ourselves second-guessing their overtures of affection?

It is true that we come to the subject of intimacy wounded, and we are hoping that someone has the secret for negotiating the mine-fields of modern relationships, some way of surviving with the fewest fatal injuries or lingering battle memories.

Relationships are not easy. And unfortunately, a book on intimacy is not a magic pill. This is where the difficulty starts. If I take this task seriously, to learn about intimacy is to learn about me. And I'm not so sure that I will like what I see. Because the truth is that—

I want to be in relationship, but it is easier to be an island.
I want to be open and vulnerable, but it is easier to be a rock.
I want to learn how to be me, but it is easier to play out an expected role.
I want to learn to feel, fully and without reservation, but it is easier to observe and spectate.
I want to be a friend, but it is easier to be an acquaintance.
I want to learn how to receive, but it is easier to be self-sufficient.
I want to learn new truths about me, but it is easier to repeat those patterns of behavior which are familiar.
I want to be human, but it is easier to maintain a reputation.
I want to learn how to talk to God, but it is easier to learn how to talk about him.
I want to grow, but it is easier to be comfortable.
I want to learn how to listen and talk to another, but it is easier to talk at (or about) another.
I want intimacy . . . or maybe I just want security.
So I shout, "Go away, come closer!"

The Journey of Self-Exploration

I realize that no book is for everyone. So there are no pretensions here. This is no cure-all, no panacea. It's the beginning of an exploration into the confusing world of interpersonal relationships. It's an honest look at who we are in such relationships, and why we behave and choose the way we do—the signals we send, the wounds we carry, and the hopes we dream. But, like an archeological dig, this process of self-exploration takes time. It's a slow process, and it is not attractive to those hoping for a quick fix or instant discoveries.

So this is a book for anyone who is willing to begin walking through the sometimes painful process of self-discovery. It is for anyone who feels stuck in a dysfunctional relationship, where there is a secret pact that no real words are spoken for fear that the apple cart may be upended. It is for those who have been taught that emotions are not to be felt but managed. It is for those who wish to look seriously at the antenna they use to attract those around them. It is for those who realize that they have succumbed to mixed messages, "bad tapes," and illusions about intimacy, and have never been given the permission to stop and examine them. It is for those who want permission to learn to be a friend to themselves, to spend time alone, and discover how to like it.

It is a book for those who are ready for an invitation to a journey. The journey of intimacy. The journey of self-discovery. The journey of self-acceptance.

It is an open invitation to explore. To unmask. To expose. To embrace. To hope. To dance. To laugh. To smile. To meet the child within. And to celebrate.

Toward that end, this book is intended to create an environment for dialogue. To be sure, the spirits of our culture—hurry, isolation, power—are all enemies of dialogue. And it will be tempting to present intimacy in as nice and neat a package as one can find—something we can control and admire and add to our relational résumés. But nice and neat doesn't do justice to real people with real hopes and real pain, who desire someone with the courage to give them permission to be fully alive, even in their incompleteness. For in this culture of relational casualties and pervasive adversaries to self-worth, we need to begin to paint an honest picture where life cannot be made trivial, where our "humanness" need not be an embarrassment, where intimacy is possible but not cheap, and where hope is not only the possession of dreamers.

Welcome to the journey.

PART I

An Invitation

"One way to express the spiritual crisis of our time is to say that most of us have an address but cannot be found there."

Henri Nouwen

1 Intimacy: Is Anyone Home?

John sat next to me on the park bench shaking his head, hoping that through our conversation some sense of enlightenment would come, and he wouldn't be so confused about his relationships. "I just don't know," he kept saying.

It was not a new theme for John, and his persistent fight with his weight indicated an ongoing struggle with self-esteem. In other conversations, he had admitted that it might have been his way of avoiding the possibility of getting close to another person.

He went on. "I'm 33 years old. And I just can't find anyone who fits. Do you know what I mean?"

I nodded.

"I mean, I'm dating three women now. But none of them have exactly what I'm looking for. I really like Carol, for example. But she prefers fun to a more serious conversation. And she's really young. I just don't want to commit to the wrong one. Oh well, I guess there's nothing you could say that would make my choices any easier."

Secretly, he hoped I would. But he was right. I wonder whether the issues had anything to do with the three women.

We want to be connected. At least a part of us does. But at the same time, we want to be an island. So we sing along with Simon and Garfunkel, "If I'd never loved, I never would have cried . . ." It is just too true, that caring leaves us vulnerable to hurt and disappointment—even rejection. The resulting self-protection so characteristic of our time is not surprising. That such a posture would be considered stock interpersonal fare, however, makes one wonder. It appears that we live in a world where detachment is the only way we survive.

So which is it? To give and receive. Or to protect and defend? To invite. Or to fend off and push away? To trust. Or to hedge our bets? To commit. Or to evade? Intimacy. Or survival? The tension exists in us all.

Henri Nouwen says that this tension shows in our restlessness. We're not at home, he says. I find that very unsettling, because it is too true. Even more unsettling is my first response to such insight: namely, guilt. Or some impulsive need to take care of it. Or some surge of will power determined to solve the problem and make things right.

Our look at intimacy begins with a recognition of our restlessness. That may be a surprise to some. What we ail must recognize, however, is that there can be two ways to approach this realization about our ongoing tension. In the first approach, our feelings of pessimism, or discouragement and gloom, even hopelessness, are only compounded by the belief that there is, in fact, something fundamentally "wrong" with us in the light of Nouwen's truth that we are not "at home." This view is predicated on the belief that the tension itself should be resolved. Or, at least avoided, if not ignored (which is the option many of us take, "Can't we go on to another subject?"). Somehow, according to this first approach, the restlessness of which Nouwen speaks cannot be instructive in any way, but only an indictment—of what we should be. Consequently, we look for proscriptions from an expert, directions from a guru, some easy-to-apply Bible verse, or some applicable fix, to liberate us from our dilemma.

"So I'm restless . . ." the modern mind reluctantly concedes. "Why can't it be fixed?"

I've come to believe, however, that the notion that such anxiety—or restlessness, or tension—can be (or even should be) completely eliminated or resolved, is based upon a naive assumption that life is just around the next corner. It assumes a destination mentality: that we arrive somewhere, and our job is to get there as quickly as possible. Consequently, today is only a preview, we seem to tell ourselves—a dress rehearsal to learn our lines and walk through the paces that will allow us to someday "get it right."

Is this, however, the only approach to our restlessness?

Embracing My Restlessness

Coming to terms with our restlessness. That's what's at stake. Granted, this seems to be a strange place to begin a book on intimacy. And yet ironically, it's been my discovery that any journey toward connectedness—or intimacy, relationship, friendship, community—must begin with a reflective look at our restlessness, which includes our discomfort, the inner contradictions ("go away . . . come closer!"), and the ambiguity.

Why? Because regardless of the definition we may choose, intimacy involves the journey toward what it means to be fully human—which means to be a participant in life, and not a spectator. Like it or not, this involves embracing the full range of emotions and ambiguities—and restlessness—we bring to the task.

Here's where our problem begins, of course. We'd rather see intimacy, vulnerability, and becoming real as proscriptive multiple-choice answers to magazine test questions—an implicit and cerebral acknowledgment that we do indeed know the "right words," but are uncomfortable digging beneath the layer of our present categories for life. There is the secret hope that the issue of intimacy can be treated as a left-brain activity, and can be resolved cognitively by adding another dose of information and correct definitions—whichever the newest book or self-help lecture can offer. We say we want intimacy, but in reality, we long for a place of stability and security.

But if it is stability that we want, our quest for intimacy will ultimately be short-circuited.

Looking at the subject of intimacy is threatening. It means probing. Asking questions that will challenge our predetermined categories. Coming face to face with our restlessness—as well as our drivenness, our ambitions and motivations, our fear, our self-consciousness, our propensity toward addictive relationships, our need to belong and our need to be needed. O God, where are the "Five easy steps to intimacy" when we need them? This honest look at restlessness is not what we had in mind!

The Search for Meaning

Our restlessness, however discouraging a subject, is not just an arbitrary idiosyncrasy granted to Americans. It's a symptom of a larger issue: namely, our persistent search—as humans—for meaning. Harold Kushner's insight underlines the issue when he writes, "I am convinced that it is not the fear of death, of our lives ending, that haunts our sleep so much as the fear that our lives will not have mattered, that as far as the world is concerned, we might as well never have lived. What we miss in our lives, no matter how much we have, is that sense of meaning" (Kushner, p. 20). To which we might add, or sense of connectedness—or intimacy.

Various illustrations come to mind. "I want to go to the place where everybody knows my name," says a current popular song. Yes! Something inside of each of us responds to this desire.

It was a few years ago when I received some insight about my own journey on this search for meaning. I was visiting a Benedictine monastery in the high desert of Southern California. My afternoon jog took me by a school bus making its final round of the day. It was stopped, and as I jogged by, a young boy jumped off and began walking the same road that I was to take.

"Hey, mister," he shouted, "can I jog with you?" His impertinence, though typical of a boy his age, was coupled with a winsome smile. I wasn't in a hurry—so I nodded and he joined in, which also provided a convenient excuse to slow the pace. Within five minutes I was given pretty much his whole life story. His name was Matthew, he was ten years old, precocious and full of life.

Abruptly, however, he stopped. "Look at this," he ordered as he showed me an 8 1/2 by 11 piece of paper that had been laminated. In big black letters across the top it said, "Fourth Grade Math Whiz." Underneath was his name, the school name, the date and the teacher's signature.

His pride was undaunted. "I'm a math whiz," he went on beaming, not waiting for me to come to that conclusion by reading the card only inches from my face. "Last year my sister was the math whiz," he continued, "but this year, I'm the math whiz!"

"That's great," I offered.

"Yep. But you know what's really great? When I get home, my dad's gonna be real proud."

I stopped. I was three times his age and still doing what he was doing. Only I was more sophisticated, and the stakes were higher, and the awards were given on a better quality of paper—framed, of course. Waiting for someone to acknowledge my achievements—my math whiz cards—and hoping that the consequent smile of affirmation would confirm my greatest hope, that "I really am somebody!"

Why does such a story about a ten-year-old boy ring true for the ten-year-old in all of us? Because each of us is bent toward meaning. Because being human means being susceptible to this infection of purpose. Why? Because we are created beings, capable of investment—creatures endowed with meaning. Created to be fully alive. To be whole. To be integrated—fully human. To be real.

This is the good news—and the amusing irony—of our tension and restlessness, that we surely miss if we are intent on an immediate solution (or obsessed with earning enough math whiz cards). It is the good news that it is possible—and even necessary—to begin our journey by allowing our restlessness to be instructive. Our restlessness as teacher? Can it be? And if so, what does it teach us about who we are?

Restlessness—Our Teacher?

This certainly doesn't sound like good news, we still want to protest.

We are restless. Granted. And we are not comfortable with our restlessness. On the one hand, we're confronted with our need to be at home, our need to be fully alive, our need to be connected. On the other hand, such need frightens us. True again.

However—is our restlessness a teacher? Or is it really an impediment, to be overcome?

To embrace our restlessness is to say to ourselves, "It's okay to begin the journey here. I don't need to pretend that I'm beyond the tension. And in embracing this restlessness, I can affirm that I was created to find wholeness and meaning and connectedness." It is the permission to begin this journey toward intimacy with a healthy dose of gentleness toward oneself. It is the permission to seek meaning without expecting to be rescued. It is the permission to embrace the journey without needing to achieve merit by arriving at some predetermined destination. For it is when we can't embrace our restlessness—our frustrations, our push-me pull-me drama—and when we lack this gentleness, that we seek a shortcut. We seek some escape. *Is there any way to short-circuit the process?* we wonder. And off we go, to find a pill, or a drug, or a hobby, or a new self-help book, or to revive some well-worn math whiz card, to eliminate the tension.

This restlessness has been given a variety of names. It is a longing in each of us to be more than he/she is, a longing which is in fact, says Carl Jung, a religious urge. For the "human psyche strives always toward wholeness, strives to complete itself and become more conscious" (R. Johnson, *We,* p. 3). Or, if you will, we strive to become more fully alive, or present, or real. The Bible talks about restoring the image of God—the image of our Creator—in Christlikeness. Andrew Greeley calls it the quest for "gentle love and for the gentle lover in oneself" (Greeley, *Confessions,* p. 22). Legends speak of the quest for the "Holy Grail." Victor Frankl calls it our longing for "transcendence," which he says has been repressed, and though "concealed in the 'transcendent unconscious' . . . transcendence shows up and makes itself noticeable as an 'unrest of the heart'" (Frankl, *The Unconscious God,* p. 68). And St. Augustine says in a prayer to God that surely, "our hearts are restless, until they find their rest in Thee."

Like it or not, we all join in this pursuit of meaning. Some of us by default, some of us driven, some of us with full awareness of our need for math whiz cards, some of us with an eye on the final destination, and some of us in an attempt to short-cut the process by learning all the right answers—always susceptible to the very American mentality that the tension can be reduced to an equation. Our task, we ask? To find the formula, our culture responds.

Feeling blue?
Buy some clothes.
Feeling lonely?
Turn on the radio.
Feeling despondent?
Read a funny book.
Feeling bored?
Watch TV.
Feeling empty?

Eat a sundae.
Feeling worthless?
Clean the house.
Feeling sad?
Tell a joke.
Ain't this modern age wonderful?
You don't gotta feel nothin',
There's a substitute for everythin'!
God have mercy on us!

—*Lois A. Cheney*

This all points to our need to short-cut and sidestep. That's the issue here, isn't it? We don't want a book about the journey of intimacy. We want magic.

Single and attractive and discouraged. Those are the words to describe Kelly, a twenty-eight-year-old part-time student, part-time waitress. "I really want someone to love," she began, "but I must do something to push people away. What is it? I wish I could figure it out. So sometimes I think, *What's the use?* I don't even want to try anymore."

She stopped a minute, and decided to be a little braver in expressing her feelings, "Sometimes I'd like to just use someone for two or three months. You know, someone who would love me just for being me. But there wouldn't have to be a commitment to complicate things, or scare them off. Then after we find the right people to commit to, we could just say goodbye."

She stopped again, "But maybe that wouldn't work."

There exists the hope for magic. As a result, we flock to self-improvement programs (80 percent of us, or so says the *Los Angeles Times*), join churches, take EST, learn yoga, practice self-hypnosis, get married, and have parties. What we receive from these programs, secular or religious, is the illusion of self-improvement, the feeling that we are now more likeable, therefore certain to be more successful. Underneath it all, we long to create a new family. To fill the void. To find the right answers. It all seems more palatable than the invitation to recognize that restlessness may be an ongoing part of the journey, and our first step is self-acceptance. Perhaps we've never been given that permission.

It's true. Henri Nouwen is right. We do have an address and still cannot be found there. But is this just an indictment, or an invitation? Is our restlessness a curse? Or a gift? Or the permission to embrace where we are . . . right now (with all of the urges and needs we bring to the task), without the need to short-cut, or repair the cracks with some new-found relational superglue.

> "I share my experience of love not as an expert but an amateur, not because I know the answers but because the question has lodged itself in me."
>
> *Sam Keen*

2 Intimacy: The Journey

It's been said that people who talk a lot about intimacy in their own lives usually don't have it.

I agree. And if I'm honest, that could be intimidating. Or embarrassing. I could feel exposed. Or unmasked. Perhaps even an impostor. Or worse yet, undeserving. But I suspect that when it comes to the subject of intimacy, we all feel those things—from time to time. And probably more often than we like to admit. Such feelings are, ironically, healthy and necessary. For it's these glimpses of vulnerability that tell us the journey of intimacy is possible.

More than ever, I'm convinced that the journey is worth taking, and that even our feelings of pain and humiliation can be a part of that journey. Also, these perils of intimacy help "show us how powerless we are in the most intimate, most rewarding moments of our lives" (D. Hassel, *Dark Intimacy,* p. 74). In other words, we don't need to run from our past, or call it a waste, or spend all our energy on our emotional defense budget. For with strange irony (even without a clear understanding or definition of this experience we call intimacy), we are innately aware that it is in the very moment of our powerlessness—of being "out of control," of having been given over to the "other," of catching a glimpse of something bigger than our worries and our pettiness, of having someone see us as we really are, of that momentary rush of freedom that comes when you utter the words, "I need you"—that we have any possibility of understanding intimacy. Only in such places of vulnerability can we touch the real self, or embrace real emotions, or see need as a genuine imperative, or break down the cyclical aloneness of protective self-sufficiency.

It means that through our weaknesses we become strong. Our weaknesses—our places of vulnerability—become signposts to our precious and indispensable humanity.

To be candid, I began with the hope that I could write a book from the vantage point of expertise. Or even success. We are all attracted to "how to" manuals, and I no less than others yearn for the stability and comfort that comes from answers. It was in the writing of—or should I say, in the difficulty in writing—this book, however, that my own perspective was altered.

There's no doubt that intimacy is an intriguing subject matter. And compelling. Without even defining it, it attracts interest. Heads tilt and ears tune in to the possibility of gleaning insights into the perplexing dilemma of human relationships (a dilemma from which none of us can completely escape). We have conveniently capsulized all this into the teaching notes for "Intimacy 101."

Actually, however, we're all in the same boat; we'd like someone to step forward and unravel the complexities of human relationships—or to at least pretend that they have the answers we need. It was something that I read from Sam Keen that helped. He said, "I share my experience of love not as an expert but an amateur, not because I know the answers but because the question has lodged itself in me" (*Passionate Life*, p. 29).

Something deep inside me said, "Yes."

My own journey reintroduced itself with a new passion. The subject at hand—intimacy, the embracing of life, the invitation to be fully human—was worth seeking even though not readily reduced to proscriptions and answers. I became convinced that the journey is important for each of us, regardless of expertise. The search itself is enough. I agree with Rabbi Levine, we may not have all the answers, but we are learning to "ask the right questions."

When stripped of mystery, life and intimacy are somehow cheapened, covered with polyester, and bargained off as a birthright for a pot of porridge. And as I look back over my relatively short life, the temptation to seek answers, theologize, compartmentalize, and proscribe is strong but ultimately empty. I look at my journey that passed through an early marriage, a divorce, a troubled single life, a remarriage, loss of a child, a confrontation with my own addictions and obsessions, a painful awareness of the reality of what it means to be an adult child of an alcoholic, and the relentless emotional reminders of the reality of a "lost childhood."

Yes, I would rather be an "expert."

There's a story about a well-traveled treacherous mountain road. It was infamous for its hair-pin turns, narrow passes, and sheer shoulders. In fact, many people, journeying to the top, failed to negotiate the road and plunged to the valley below. In response to these tragedies, the community decided to build a hospital. It was located in the valley, at the bottom of the mountain, and very accessible to crash victims. Over the years, the hospital received much business, and flourished. One day, a newcomer came to town and suggested that the money spent in hospital maintenance could be better spent providing maps, and placing signs and warnings and guard rails along the mountain road.

I hope that this book can do the same. I know with certainty that this road toward intimacy is an ongoing journey of identifying and uncovering the land-mines and potholes that crowd the pathway. More than anything else, we simply need permission—an ongoing nudge, a word of encouragement, another person standing by as advocate, a story of inspiration, somebody in my corner of the ring with a sponge of water and a kind word, a reminder—to keep on the journey, to "keep on keeping on." We need the ongoing affirmation that the journey is ultimately worth pursuing . . . for its own sake.

I hope that this book can be such a permission—to ask questions, to search, to doubt, to probe, to feel, to enjoy, to laugh, to cry, to wonder—and to feel the wonder of what it means to embrace the journey toward becoming fully human. I hope it provides a clear picture of the road hazards along the way. In the words of Sam Keen, "As a fledgling, I have little knowledge about high flying, but I can offer some advice about how to flap your wings and fall from high places with a minimum of injury" (Keen, *Passionate Life,* p. 29).

Sharing as a fledgling is no easy task, however. How exactly does one go about this process of disclosure for the purpose of learning, without simply airing dirty laundry, or elevating failures, or becoming lost in the maze of what is lost, at the expense of what may be gained?

Two Foundational Themes

Let's begin this journey with an awareness of two foundational themes within each of us.

On the one hand, *we cannot live completely isolated.* We need touch. We need attention. We need conversation. We need someone to listen. We need warmth and affection. We need to be needed. It is true—as one author noted, that, "one chimpanzee is not a chimpanzee." Even more so, one human being cannot be human. We are "bent" toward relationships. Without even defining the word, we yearn for intimacy. We are people who need people. And yet, sometimes, we feel as if we're trying to convince ourselves that such a statement is true. (Why does it seem so easy to believe when Barbra Streisand sings about the "luckiest people in the world"?)

In a poignant illustration from the TV mini-series based upon James Michener's *Centennial,* we see our ongoing tension between relationship and isolation. A wagoner pulled into town with his Conestoga wagon, jumped off the seat, and with an outburst of anger and resignation announced, "I'm through. I'm done. Do you want this wagon? It's yours." The young man to whom the comments were addressed looked puzzled. He clearly didn't understand. The old man standing nearby explained.

"He gave up his bells. When a teamster breaks down and has to accept help from another teamster he has to give up his brass bells. It's a sign he needed help and couldn't make it alone. Making it alone, that's what life on the road is all about."

Why does such an illustration ring true?

It's because on the other hand—and with equal certainty—*we know that needing people hurts.* To build relationships—or intimacy—requires that I give me, or at least a part of me. That's too close to home. In his autobiography, Andrew Greeley comments, "I am under no illusion that life need continue to be relatively peaceful. We are all fragile. We can be easily hurt by chance and/or by the malevolence of those who don't like us. I learned during the late seventies and early eighties that Murphy's law is fundamentally sound: anything can go wrong anytime" (Greeley, *Confessions,* p. 497).

We've all taken that first step away from isolation, and we've paid the price.

We've run to join in the playground fun, only to find ourselves standing alone—picked last for kickball. We've waited by the door—football in hand—waiting for Dad to arrive and make good his morning promise to come home early for a "little game of catch," only to realize that Dad forgot.

While at the prom, we've seen our dream/fantasy woman smile assuredly on the arm of the football player who stands head and shoulders above us—not only in stature, but in charm, looks, and "potential." Or we've been that football player (or cheerleader) and basked in the attention and limelight, while at the same time feeling a pang of loneliness—wondering if we'll get all this attention when the superstar role has faded.

We've married in good faith—hoping against hope that our marriage would be different—only to find that familiarity does breed contempt. And we take and are taken for granted. We have wondered how something which began so good—bathed in mutual adoration, devotion and passion—could end up so destructive, enveloped and clouded in mistrust and even hatred. How can you loathe someone you once loved (and perhaps still love)? We mull the question over and over in our minds, hoping against hope that the answer will come out right. And some have been "lucky enough" to have been "rescued" from an unbearable marriage (or other significant relationship), by someone who "really" cares, and listens and loves. Only later do we discover that the magic ends when the laundry gets dirty, and that in the end we may have lost not only what we had (but at the time didn't want), but also what we thought we needed—and maybe even ourselves.

I pray in faith—honestly believing that God is there (or at least is listening)—only to find my prayers greeted by what appears to be a deafening silence. I've worked hard to be a good Christian, and kept my nose clean, only to discover that morality is a lousy bargaining chip if what I wanted was a better or easier life—and that God doesn't seem to love me any better because of my medals. I make friends who misinterpret me, or who become too busy, or who seem to be too easily hurt—or are too much like me. And I have—in a state of disbelief—watched friends take information that has been both personal and confessional, and use it against me. It may be a pejorative act, or maybe just a misunderstanding. But knowing the reason does little to lessen the pain.

We are reminded of the time and energy we have invested in friendships that have slowly disintegrated due to lack of time, or distance. We have stood in airports (or train stations, or driveways) to say goodbye to someone significant, trying not to feel the real impact of loss, regardless of how it is soothed with the reassuring words, "We'll keep in touch. We'll write soon. We'll call." And something deep inside us begins to harden. To want to protect. To want to keep safe. To want to avoid another replay of the same storyline.

We've had someone care for us—really care. And it takes us off guard, for no performance on our part was required. And we wondered when it was going to end and whether it was really an act. This experience has led some of us to sabotage the relationship before it sabotaged us.

We stood at the side of a crib that holds a miracle, and our minds and hearts are full of dreams, hopes, plans—and pride, and an awareness of emotions that over the years have been for the most part covered, or forgotten, or denied. Our child! Then we watched the years slip by, measuring them by missed opportunities. We realize that the "miracle" grows up and away from our control, and we painfully realize that miracles, like love, cannot be controlled.

All too many of us, raised in the precarious environment of an alcoholic (or addictive, or substance abuse, or dysfunctional) home have absorbed and internalized—without complete understanding or evaluation—the ongoing double messages of "I love you, go away," or "You don't really amount to much, but I need you," or "You can't really please me, but don't you dare stop trying." And we're confronted as adults by the all too persistent pattern with which we handle relationships, with our self-worth tied to our need to rescue or manage or fix someone else, while at the same time we are in the dark about our own needs, feelings, wants, and desires.

Then we wake up one morning—and look at the reflection in the mirror—and we realize we are not who we had wanted to become. For before us is the sobering truth of our propensity toward being inhuman: isolated, selfish, unforgiving, cruel—or maybe just indifferent, apathetic, and detached, selectively compassionate and sometimes bigoted. And we realize that most of it is protective. This is not out of calculation. Or cruelty. It is out of fear.

And yet we open the door of our lives once again—to our family, friends, spouse, children—and shout with open arms, "Go away, closer!" (cf. Hassell, *Dark Intimacy*).

The truth is, relationships hurt. And it seems that history is full of the rubble of unkept promises, broken communities, and shattered alliances.

We want out. But not yet. Someday—we're convinced—we'll "get it right." It will all make sense. We'll get our act together. We'll learn enough to love the people closest to us. Or, we'll finally meet the right person. Or our parents and family will finally change, finally grow up. Or enough time will pass, and our past will no longer haunt our present attempts at relationships.

Or "she" (or is it he?) will make me intimate. She will never leave.

Someday.

But, someday never seems to come.

Relationships: A Risk in an Imperfect World

More than ever, we need the permission to live today—to take the next step. We need permission to believe that relationships are ultimately worth it. That we can, in confidence, take the first steps toward connections, knowing full well the cost. We need permission to risk—to not settle for solely functional relationships. And we need permission to know that—dream as we may—relationships will never be perfect—that "relationships are at best imperfect connections" (Viorst, *Necessary Losses*).

At the same time, we need the freedom to choose healthy relationships, relationships that are good for us. We need permission to look honestly at the mixed messages we send, and the games we play. We need permission to look squarely in the face of our bundle of idiosyncrasies and fault lines, and embrace ourselves—for who we are, and not for who we should be.

If we don't look, we walk blindly, destined to repeat the same mistakes.

Together we will walk the journey of learning to risk in an imperfect world, learning to uncover the survival mechanisms that we use to avoid closeness with others. We have permission to learn slowly to let go of the past, and the permission to begin to forgive an imperfect world. Together we begin to learn new road signs that may keep us from plunging into unhealthy alliances, assuming that the hospital will always be there to patch us up.

Too often, we plunge into relationships, hoping for the best. Probably we fear looking at our vulnerability. We are all afraid of the shadow-side—the brokenness. Nowhere is that more apparent than with the subject of intimacy. Neither our trivialization nor our sophistication has eliminated our fear of being exposed. We want to be real, to understand intimacy, to give and receive love. At the same time we fear nakedness, vulnerability, and incompleteness. We want to be intimate, *but can't I wait until I've got my "act together"?* we wonder.

I'm convinced that the answer to this approach-avoidance dilemma cannot lie in more precise definitions, as if intimacy is something we can possess. The answer must lie in our ability to live with ambiguity and the possibility that intimacy is slowly uncovered without the need to remove the mysteries of life and without the need to repress the shadow-side.

In other words, there is no need for any magic wands here, although it would certainly be easier.

It's a lesson a small rabbit learned in a nursery toy room. Maybe it fits for us too.

> "Does it hurt?" asked the Rabbit.
>
> "Sometimes," said the Skin Horse, for he was always truthful. "When you are Real you don't mind being hurt."

"Does it happen all at once, like being wound up," he asked, "or bit by bit?"

"It doesn't happen all at once," said the Skin Horse. "You become. It takes a long time. That's why it doesn't often happen to people who break easily, or have sharp edges, or who have to be carefully kept. Generally, by the time you are Real, most of your hair has been loved off, and your eyes drop out and you get loose in the joints and very shabby. But these things don't matter at all, because once you are Real you can't be ugly, except to people who don't understand."

The Rabbit sighed. He thought it would be a long time before this magic called Real happened to him. He longed to become Real, to know what it felt like; and yet the idea of growing shabby and losing his eyes and whiskers was rather sad. He wished that he could become it without these uncomfortable things happening to him (M. Williams, *The Velveteen Rabbit*).

The uncomfortable things are the demons that undoubtedly will rise in any process of self-discovery. And there will be three choices with the demons we will face on this journey to become real. We can deny them, or we can attempt to defeat them, or we can slowly let them out, and learn to tame them.

"Millions of people waste vast amounts of energy desperately and futilely attempting to make the reality of their lives conform to the unreality of the myth."

Scott Peck

"We live in a crazy world and the only way to see it properly is to stand permanently on your head."

G. K. Chesterton

3 Intimacy: The Counterfeits

"When I use a word," Humpty Dumpty informed Alice, "it means precisely what I want it to mean, nothing more, nothing less."

I wish it were that simple with the word intimacy. But the agenda has already been determined by the world in which we live. We cannot begin this subject with the naive assumption that intimacy can be neatly defined or contained.

We have a semantical problem. The White House speaks of *intimate dinners* for 300. Our preachers warn us against *premarital intimacy*. Fredericks of Hollywood sells *intimate apparel*. And *Redbook* offers quizzes on developing *intimacy skills*.

There are two ways to strip a word of its meaning. One, you can confine it by significant restrictions (for example, the term pro-life). Or, two, you can banalize it by overgeneralization (for example, the words love and intimacy). As a catch-all word, intimacy has been defined, analyzed, debated, and inserted into Harlequin novels. And in the process it's been depersonalized. We've removed the edge. Intimacy has been domesticated. We can now possess intimacy without it requiring anything from us.

Our first task in this journey, then, is not one of learning, but of unlearning. All the blue ribbon definitions in the world will do us no good, if we continue to walk through life, restricted by some illusion. To move forward, intimacy must be rescued from the illusions—which we have created—that shackle it. Whether we like it or not, each of us has been susceptible to some imitation of intimacy that promises glitter and in the end, cruelly disappoints.

Our secret hope, still, is that understanding will release us from any tension. So we seek helpful and succinct definitions. We go to lectures. We buy tapes. And we read books. Maybe they will tell us what we need to know, we presume. If we can walk away with a few well-worded definitions, we are satisfied. With our new insights conveniently contained and attractively displayed in the seminar three-ring binder, somehow, intimacy is more manageable. Or at least less ominous. Less frightening. Information becomes a bargaining chip, like an added prize or math whiz card. And, if all else fails (our subconscious reasoning tells us), we can use the knowledge of precise and suitable definitions which we now possess as a weapon. One of the easiest ways for us to avoid our own fear and need for growth is to project our shortcomings onto others. I can do that under the guise of "helpful information." "Look what I know"—and therefore, "look what I can tell you to help you change in your life"—too often becomes the substitute for personal incorporation, struggle, and admission of need.

There's the illusion of power and control when we think we've defined any given thing. It gives us the feeling of closure. The irony, of course, is that the fertile ground of intimacy is vulnerability (or powerlessness). Vulnerability is a stance of openness. Closure (or control) is its antithesis. In this journey toward intimacy it will be important for us to identify those ways in which we try to bring closure, to look at the counterfeit intimacies to which we are all susceptible. If that's the case, then, our initial task is not to define intimacy (or bring closure), but to free it from unrealistic and misleading definitions. Growth and change are not just a matter of adding to (more information, more insight, etc.), but stripping away that which may be false or unhealthy.

Our Equation of Real with Useful

Our problem begins with the fact that we believe our American culture when it tells us that "more is never enough." As a consequence, our perception of what is "real" is distorted. In our culture, something is real because it has market value. It is a potential commodity. It is useful. It has pragmatic applications.

Thomas Merton provides a helpful analogy. Sitting alone in the woods with his Coleman lantern, he is confronted with the fact that Coleman has constructed its lantern with a pragmatic intention over and above the simple provision of light. The packing box declares that the lantern, "stretches days to give more hours of fun." Merton asks rhetorically, "Can't I just be in the woods without any special reason?" He goes on to say that, in fact, "We are not having fun, we are not 'having' anything, we are not 'stretching our days,' and if we had fun it would not be measured by hours. Though as a matter of fact that is what fun seems to be: a state of diffuse excitation that can be measured by the clock and 'stretched' by an appliance" (*Raids,* pp. 13–14).

In such a state (where real is defined by pragmatic commodities), we are no longer free. Life—and relationships—can no longer be celebrated. They can only be overcome, or conquered by definition, or provided meaning by propitious use—or in some way manipulated to be pragmatic.

Consequently, we are prone to wonder in any given relationship, *Of what value is it to me now?* Or, *What do they do for me?* Or, *Do they make me happy?* Or, *If it is of no value, why keep it?*

With this illusion about reality, we begin to wage war on the wrong front. Intimacy—like other issues involving personal growth—becomes externalized.

It is this obsessiveness that in turn prevents us from touching true intimacy (or, our true selves), for we tend to view intimacy from our perch of control—the detachment that comes from knowledge, where life is nice and neat, where the other person is always the one with the problem, and where two plus two always equals four. The formula always works out. The relationship always produces the intended result. We want our relationships like we want our Hondas. The ad says boldly, "Fall in love without paying the price . . . The Honda Civic Hatchback is a lot like everyone's ideal. It makes you happy, without making a lot of demands."

We will gain a better perspective on the battle at hand when we understand our enemies. What are the obstacles that prevent us from coming face-to-face with ourselves? What are the illusions we carry that allow us the luxury of detachment and distance by "understanding"? What are the misconceptions that short-circuit our attempts at true self-disclosure and genuine trust? What is there in us that seeks to redefine love and intimacy in terms that are easier to swallow?

We must be quick to point out, however, that in this attraction to counterfeit intimacy, there is not necessarily an aim to deceive. More realistically, it is our need to protect what is known against what is unknown. This is a move not of calculation or cruelty, but of fear, the fear of exchanging comfort for growth—à la the Velveteen Rabbit—and of exchanging security for maturation.

The Need to Hide from Weakness

Our real self (or intimacy) is avoided and a counterfeit self is exposed. It is no wonder that certain subjects become taboo in our culture: such as death, sex, God, and one's soul.

Why? Because such subjects threaten our ability to be in control. They confront us with our humanity—our vulnerability, our aloneness, and our need. We realize that in the midst of our sophistication, we are still like boys and girls in a department store at Christmas: given to fantasy and infatuation and jealousy, mixed with just enough fear from a vengeful Santa. By the same token, we of necessity avoid the confrontation with real presence that comes from silence, dwelling (or, living with, in order to really see), and death. And we construct a world view that is manageable and seemingly less threatening. If we can contain life (by closure in areas of intimacy, relationships, etc.), we can stay reasonably convinced about our being-in-control. And we can—at least partially—avoid the inevitable confrontation with our frailty, our weakness, our nakedness, our passion, our aloneness, and our slavery.

In Hugh Hefner, the *Playboy* magnate, we see a graphic illustration of our constant intentional construction of a protective illusion against vulnerability—and therefore our brokenness. In a *Newsweek* interview, we learn that "Hefner has managed to get through countless liaisons without ever getting near the altar. At 60, he estimates that he has slept with 'about a thousand women' and still hasn't reconciled himself to conjugal captivity. 'I'm probably becoming more romantic,' he says, adding with a knowing grin, 'I haven't had too many lonely nights over the last 30 years.' The bunnymaster still believes in innocence—especially his own" (*Newsweek,* "The Bunnymaster and His Many Mistresses," 8/4/86, p. 55).

In the same way—with our lives—without facing the counterfeit intimacies that tempt us, we perpetuate a lie. Granted, this may be with no real need to deceive, but the outcome is the same: inauthenticity. I deceive myself into believing that I am participating in something, which in fact I am purposely avoiding. Out of cruelty or calculation? No. Out of fear? Yes.

Consequently, it is no longer a matter of just learning correct definitions, or of mastering the skill of casual party chatter guaranteed to attract a member of the opposite sex, or of being recognized for our ability to listen and empathize, or of scoring high on the latest intimacy quiz featured in the newest edition of our favorite magazine. In fact, it is not nearly as easy as all that. This journey of intimacy, or of becoming real, begins with a difficult admission. "We become free," Ray Anderson reminds us, "to the extent that we own and accept that we are not free" (Anderson, *On Being Human,* p. 94). In the words of the above Hefner analogy, we become free to the extent that we own and accept that we are no longer innocent.

This is the first step of our growth. Of change. To go home, we must admit we're away. To diet, we must admit that ice cream is easier to swallow. To learn intimacy, we must face the counterfeit intimacies to which we cling.

What are these counterfeits? And why is this step so difficult? They are addictions and compulsions ("more is never enough"), greed ("I'm in a hurry"), and well-constructed illusions about intimacy and authentic relationships ("we were intimate last night") which erect a barrier to our true self and therefore to the possibility of true dialogue.

Such images are built on faulty belief systems—or faulty equations if you will. In our need for closure and comfort we are susceptible to any number of interludes or experiences that will complete the sentence, "Intimacy is. . ."

A Look at the Counterfeits

Our journey begins with this cost of unlearning, with an honest look at our faulty belief systems. Below are some of the counterfeits that so easily tempt us. What is the price we must pay for facing them? The sacrifice of comfort and illusion.

Intimacy is always ecstasy. In our Madison Avenue culture, we are bombarded daily—via TV, radio, magazines, billboards and the like (not to mention T-shirts and bumper stickers)—with the dictum: If you are living life right, you are "up" most of the time. You are "happening." You are "together." You are "in." Even, you are "bad"—meaning very good.

It is a perspective of reality—that consequently infects and affects our relationships.

This counterfeit intimacy is our way of being both everywhere and nowhere. The result, of course, is intentional. We do not have to truly encounter or be encountered. We can opt for mingling. We can replace engagement with networking. We can replace authenticity with excitement and performance. We can replace silence with noise. We can replace a boring Saturday night alone with a promise of fun. And we can replace affection with an all-essential orgasm.

What's the payoff? What's the attraction? This illusion of ecstasy—accompanied by our busy, hurried lifestyle—is helpful. It keeps us from something threatening, something frightening. One thirty-two-year-old man told me about his frequent jaunts to Lake Tahoe "for pleasure." The weekend encounters—with a variety of women—were frequent and went on for about two years. "How could you maintain the pace?" I asked. "Oh," he replied, "it always remained exciting. We never saw each other long enough to get bored."

Maybe that's it. We're afraid to be bored. Why? Because then we must face ourselves. Then we are no longer protected by the trinkets—by the ecstasy that dulls the throbbing of my inner loneliness. Boredom—says Victor Frankl—points us to our "existential vacuum." It points to our fear of being alone, and our need to collect relationships to rescue us from that tension.

This counterfeit is echoed in the words of a single woman in an affair with a married man: "It didn't have to deteriorate because of having to be in a day-to-day domestic situation where demands are made on each other that are unpleasant or mundane. It was never mundane. It was encapsulated" (from the *New Other Woman).*

This philosophy comes even from the rich and the famous. Said one actress, "Ecstasy has not been rare in my life, but when the ecstasy is gone, I am gone too. I never can stay longer than the ecstasy."

This fear is illustrated in a recent description given about a very well-known author and lecturer. "It's not enough for him to be ordinary anymore," said a close friend, "I'm glad I'm not cursed with that fate."

What's at issue here is looking good. Reputation. Image. *What will people think?* we incessantly wonder. And our discomfort with ourselves spills over into our relationships, as we are easily susceptible to promises of adulation. "Let's do lunch," we say in a world no longer of friends, but of contacts and allies.

The cycle is fueled. As we are confronted with our ordinariness, and consequently our boredom, it is not enough. We must find more. The ordinary no longer titillates. It no longer excites. And the illusion that ecstasy equals intimacy only fuels the fire, a fire that eventually consumes us. It's as if we want intimacy to be pain free—and a lifestyle of ecstasy passports keeps us above the "dailiness," and therefore, the potential hurtfulness of life.

The second illusion is related to the first.

Intimacy is equated with romance. We've been conned into equating intimacy with romance. And why not? After all, in this culture, isn't romance "the grail that should reward our restlessness, the sacred fulfillment that is supposed to compensate us for profaning the world?" (Keen, p. 8). And hasn't life been reduced to the pragmatic, the useful, the productive? Haven't we been taught that it is the useful which titillates, excites, thrills, and inflames?

Have you found life to be difficult? Friends unsympathetic? Have you felt unloved, ignored, or unwanted? Are your weekends continual variations on emotional solitaire?

Romance to the rescue! It is the holy grail of our pragmatic culture.

It's been said that romance in our capitalist society is often like looking for a bargain in a department store. Missing the point of the analogy, and not to be shortchanged, we express our frustration at being late to the sale, and that we never seem to find anything to our liking nor anywhere near our size.

We're in a dilemma. Our restlessness serves as a persistent reminder of our incompleteness and our need for connectedness—or wholeness and fulfillment. But instead of seeing our restlessness—our humanity and our condition of incompleteness—as an invitation, we see it as a problem to be solved. Within the Western myth of competence as a measurement of success, we invoke a formula, or invent a technique, or create a TV show called "Love Boat." The answer, we are promised, is on the way.

Therein lies the inherent flaw with the Western myth of romance. Rather than leading us to an understanding and embracing of intimacy—of connectedness, of community, of vulnerability, of becoming real—it promises to rescue us from the process. It promises freedom from dailiness, freedom from gray skies, freedom from loneliness and alienation. We are now somebody—because we have somebody. There is an implicit and unconscious demand that the lover be the savior, the one who sets us free and the one who makes us whole.

Why? Because "when we are 'in love' we feel completed, as though a missing part of ourselves had been returned to us; we feel uplifted, as though we were suddenly raised above the level of the ordinary world. Life has an intensity, a glory, an ecstasy and transcendence. We seek in romantic love to be possessed by our love, to soar to the heights, to find ultimate meaning and fulfillment in our beloved. We seek the feeling of wholeness" (Johnson, *We,* p. 52).

This is not meant to be romance bashing. What is at stake here is not a need to repudiate romance. Romance itself is not on trial, for romance is a natural part of the human condition. It is our spontaneous and emotional and visceral response to the yearning for completeness in another person. Call it chemistry. Passion. Infatuation. Sentiment. Sensuality.

Romance is alive and well, and a good indicator that our drivenness toward relationship is not purely procreative.

Unfortunately, more is never enough.

At stake is our self-esteem. And our struggle is not waged in isolation. Earlier in the book we referred to the reality that one human is not a human. By our nature we need connection. Touch. Affirmation. Strokes. The irony is that the human condition—this restlessness that compels us toward connectedness—also propels us to seek relief. Freedom. And we exchange our contingent freedom—which is the human condition of the need for connectedness—for what we assume to be absolute freedom. The result? Slavery. Obsession. Disillusionment. And even addiction. And our disillusionment continues to fuel the fire. For we point the accusing finger at the beloved, arguing that "love let me down again." The word "love" is becoming interchangeable with "she" or "he" or "they."

Our task is becoming clear. Is it possible for us to stop and look at the counterfeits which lead us blindly along, promising wholeness and life, but are never able to completely deliver? Is it possible to face the reality that "despite our ecstasy when we are 'in love', we spend much of our time with a deep sense of loneliness, alienation, and frustration over our inability to make genuinely loving and committed relationships" (*We,* p. xii).

What gives? No magic potion?

I agree with Carl Jung when he said that "if you find the psychic wound in an individual or a people, there you also find a path to consciousness. For it is in the healing of our psychic wounds that we come to know ourselves" (*We,* p. xii).

Translation? Until I confront—or admit to, or embrace—the unreality of the counterfeits to which I sell my soul, and therefore my identity, I will continue to want to make the reality of my life conform to the unreality of such illusions. The irony is that fully comprehending true intimacy is not what is necessary here. Rather, it is our need to come face to face with our woundedness which compels us to seek refuge in an impostor intimacy. Thus our wounded psyche—which is the human condition of need and incompleteness—remains hidden, repressed, buried, and always susceptible to fool's gold. In this case, the glitter is romance.

What are we saying? That romance is to be avoided? That it has no value? Not at all. I'm not ready to give up romance quite yet. But is it possible to unshackle romance from the unrealistic expectations that accompany it? Can we learn both from our need to fall in love, and our propensity to seek a savior from life—that in the end turns out to be a tyrant? Can we unpack the excess baggage that hinders our journey? Can we come to an understanding of our need for connectedness, without needing to be consumed? Can we deal with our need for relationship, without a need to be rescued, and our need to give and receive, without becoming an addict?

The answer is yes, although the pathway is not easy. It is one of unlearning. Yes, it has been said that the "truth will set us free." But first, it will make us uncomfortably mad! For the claims and promises of the Western myth that equates romance and intimacy are pervasive and persuasive.

The Promises of Romance

Let's look at four such claims:*

- I will be a fulfilled and completed person if I am in love.

"I'm not me unless I have you" equates my identity with what I have—or earn, or compete for, or do, or consume—not with who I am. The claim is intensified if we were raised with the religious dogma that when God created us, he created one more person on the globe just for us. And our job in life is to find that person. God's job, it seems, is to play hide and seek with that person for as long as he can!

* These ideas are adapted from William Lenters, *The Freedom We Crave*, pp. 30–32. In this very helpful book William Lenters discusses the relationship between romance and addiction.

It is no wonder that in the United States, too many of us burn all other relationship bridges when we "fall in love." Why? Because now we have the one who will complete us. "Hello there, you lucky person. You get the job of spending the rest of your life making me okay!"

It appears that most of us don't have relationships, we take hostages.

This myth only serves to infect all our relationships. Merle Shain points out that, "Our society isn't very big on friendship, really. We think of friends as people to spend time with when there isn't anyone else around who really matters. And sometimes when we have a vacancy for lover or spouse, we look for someone to fill that slot instead of seeing what there is, and miss what might have been" (*When Lovers Are Friends,* p. 84).

I am in a second marriage. And I honestly believed, after my divorce, that falling in love with someone would "make me okay" again. It was accompanied by the insidious belief that I married the "wrong person" the first time around. Hence, the reason we "fell out of love." Not this time, I argued. "If only I could fall in love with the right one this time," my faulty reasoning contended, "life would be good again."

- My loneliness and sense of solitude will be taken care of only in romantic liaison with another human being.

This is, at best, a half-truth. Yes, we are creatures of relationship. But in our lifetime, we experience relationships not only as experiences of intimacy, but as experiences of loneliness. Keith Clark, a Capuchin monk, sheds some light on this tension. "Moments of intimacy are always satisfying in some way, but they are always incomplete. Even when they are very satisfying in the joy of the moment, they are incomplete in that the moment ends . . . . Moments of intimacy and moments of loneliness cannot be avoided" (p. 25, 29).

I am secretly hoping that a romantic liaison will release me from this ongoing tension. "Rescue me," I cry. The ebb and flow of relationships begins with the reality that I am ultimately alone. And the giving of myself to another embraces that aloneness. It does not deny it. I see it as a gift, not a curse.

• Connection with another human being will resolve my anxieties, my neuroses, my traumas.

And so we marry young to escape an unhappy home. We have affairs to find someone who "really cares and listens." We submerge ourselves in romance novels, waiting for our prince to carry us away. We buy books on how to restore our passion of love, hoping that some technique will release us from the continued pressure of the real and ordinary world. We transfer all our "in-loveness" to one of our children, projecting on that person the power to rescue us from the human drama, and hoping that we will ride to a more satisfying life on his or her coattails.

• Love can make me happy.

She was blond, tan, and stereotypically "Californian." Outwardly optimistic, at age 23, Laura seemed like the world was hers. Strong-willed and socially outgoing, Laura talked with certainty about her views on life. Her parents divorced at age eight, and Laura found herself without a father ("He's called me twice in the last fifteen years," she adds matter of factly). She had made a vow to never be in a relationship that ends up like that of her parents.

Now Laura is faced with what might have been. Married at age nineteen, she has now been separated from her husband for a year. She talked about her situation. "He still wants to be married, but I can't go back into a situation like that again. He doesn't drink, or hurt me, so sometimes I feel guilty for leaving. But the truth is, I'm just not happy. And you can't have a good marriage unless you're happy."

After a refill of her iced tea, she goes on. "It was one of those born-again Christian marriages when we started. But it was like I had to drag him to church. Now that we're separated, he goes every week, and he preaches to me about how what I'm doing is not in God's will. And I hate it!

"Is there someone who could love me and make me happy?"

The equation here is similar to the first claim. Someone else can make me okay. Make me happy. Make me truly alive. It means that we hope to become a victim of intimacy. Someone else can fill in the missing pieces in our lives.

The third counterfeit is connected.

Intimacy is equated with sex. In fact, we easily interchange the words.

When quizzed about her dating relationship, one coed told me, "Oh, we're doing okay, but we have not been intimate yet." Translation: "We have not yet had intercourse."

It's the same definition of intimacy used on the cover of a recent Christian book on dating that urges single people to "avoid premarital intimacy." Premarital intimacy?

The implication here, of course, is twofold: one, we assume that intimacy is somehow confirmed, or at least verified, by some genital activity. This makes our task easier. If genital use signified intimacy, we could reduce the subject to a manual of "how, when and where," becoming technicians rather than lovers. Granted, genital sexuality is certainly an expression—either positively or negatively—of our hunger and need for intimacy. But that hardly means that we can begin to equate intimacy with specific behaviors or specific sexual mores. It's such thinking that leads to the second implication that intimacy is possible, therefore, only with a member of the opposite sex, and is fueled by some romantic connection.

It's as if we don't know the language of intimacy, so we use sex.

Now the cultural equation is complete. Intimacy equals romance plus a healthy dose of sex. Somehow, intimacy is relegated to those moments when our genitals touch. This is convenient maybe, but hardly true. Ironically, it is easier for us to take our clothes off than it is to take our masks off.

It is easier to give someone our body than it is to give a part of our soul.

With such counterfeit, it is easily apparent in our sexually bombarded culture why it is difficult to talk about same sex intimacy without homophobic overtones. Again, friendship is demoted in favor of genital relationships.

The consequence is an approach to life that will objectify those around me. C. S. Lewis once said that when a man says he wants a "good woman," he really doesn't want a woman that is "good." He wants a good experience, for which the woman happens to be a necessary apparatus.

We have somehow missed the point that sexuality is far more than what one does with one's genitals. Our sexuality can be used not only to expose and disclose, but to hide and to camouflage. This is the culture, after all, observed Rollo May, that has "taken the fig leaf off our genitals and covered our faces."

Intimacy is "out there" somewhere. It is another form of "victim intimacy." It assumes that someone, or some place, or some experience, can "make us intimate." In the same way then we assume someone "makes us angry." It is a counterfeit summed up in a conversation I had with a waitress while dining at a local restaurant.

"What do you do?" she asked.

"Seminars," I replied.

"On what?"

"Relationships, mostly."

"Are you in a relationship now?" she quizzed.

I couldn't help myself. I smiled. "Yes, in fact, several of them."

She gave me a look of disbelief, and just stared for a minute to see if I was pulling her leg. Then she continued to talk, as if she needed someone to hear her plight, "I'm not in a relationship now. I'm still young. Some day maybe. And I'm waiting for the right person to come along. I haven't found him yet, but when I do. . . ."

Some day. When the right person comes along. When the

right circumstances present themselves. When I "get my act together." These will make me intimate.

And we wait. And we wait. And in the meantime, we live life with the perpetual "if only."

"If only someone really cared."
"If only I hadn't been hurt so many times before."
"If only my current set of problems were resolved."
"If only my parents weren't neurotic."
"If only she knew what a good thing she is missing."
"If only I could live yesterday again."
"If only I had more time."
"If only my kids would leave home."
"If only Dad wouldn't have drunk so much."
"If only I hadn't made Dad leave home."

Merle Shain talks about our plight. "Fulfillment is always something the other guy's got, something just over the hill. . . . So we wait in vain for something else, something just a little better than what we've got, and often we trade in the thing we have for something we think we should want" (*When Lovers Are Friends,* pp. 28–29).

We are the "who says you can't have it all?" generation, waiting for the perfect thing to commit to. We want the perfect job, the perfect house, the perfect vacation, the perfect date, the perfect child, the perfect love—and wonder about our lingering misery while we wait, failing to realize that our misery is tied to what we "should be."

The result, says Paul Tournier, is that, "We spend our entire life indefinitely preparing to live." Or, as one single mom verified with the comment, "I can't have any relationships now, my kids are still at home."

There's a reading by Robert Hutchings that fits here. It's called "The Station."

> Tucked away in our subconscious is an idyllic vision. We see ourselves on a long trip that spans the continent. We are traveling

by train. Out the windows we drink in the passing scene of cars on nearby highways, of children waving at a crossing, of cattle grazing on a distant hillside, of smoke pouring from a power plant, of row upon row of corn and wheat, of flatlands and valleys, of mountains and rolling hillsides, of city skylines and village malls.

But uppermost in our minds is the final destination. On a certain day at a certain hour we will pull into the station. Bands will be playing and flags waving. Once we get there so many wonderful dreams will come true and the pieces of our lives will fit together like a complicated jigsaw puzzle. How restlessly we pace the aisles, damning the minutes—waiting, waiting for the station.

"When we reach the station, that will be it!" we cry. "When I'm 18 . . . when I buy a new 450 SL Mercedes Benz . . . when I put the last kid through college . . . when I pay off the mortgage . . . when I get a promotion . . . when I reach the age of retirement . . . I shall live happily ever after!"

Sooner or later we must realize that there is no station, no one place to arrive at for once and for all. The true joy of life is the trip; the station is only a dream. It constantly outdistances us. For it isn't the burdens of today that drive men mad. It is the regrets over yesterday and the fear of tomorrow. Regret and fear are twin thieves who rob us of today.

So stop pacing the aisles and counting the miles. Instead, climb more mountains, eat more ice cream, go barefoot more often, swim more rivers, watch more sunsets, laugh more. . . . Life must be lived as we go along. The station will come soon enough.

(*The Station* by Robert J. Hutchings)

The message from each of these counterfeits, is that somehow, we (or our life) are not good enough, as we are now. So we spend our energy trying to complete, or fill the vacuum. We're so obsessed with what we lack, that we will attempt to force someone, or something, to fill the void. And we never see the self—our self—as whole. But only as a hole that must be filled.

And whatever we use (romance, sex, ecstasy) is never enough, of course.

Our journey toward intimacy will be the ongoing process

of "giving up." Of facing the counterfeits. Unmasking them. Of relinquishing our job as victim. Of learning to face, and accept, life as it is. No one said the process would be fun, or easy, or free from frustration and pain.

Intimacy. A journey that will cost us our innocence, our illusions, and our certainty. Somehow, I was hoping it would be different.

But then, intimacy is not a possession. It is a journey. It is not where we arrive. It is the direction we are going.

"There are two sources of unhappiness in life. One is not getting what you want; the other is getting it."

George Bernard Shaw

"Most of us don't know what we want in life, but we're sure we haven't got it."

Alfred E. Neuman

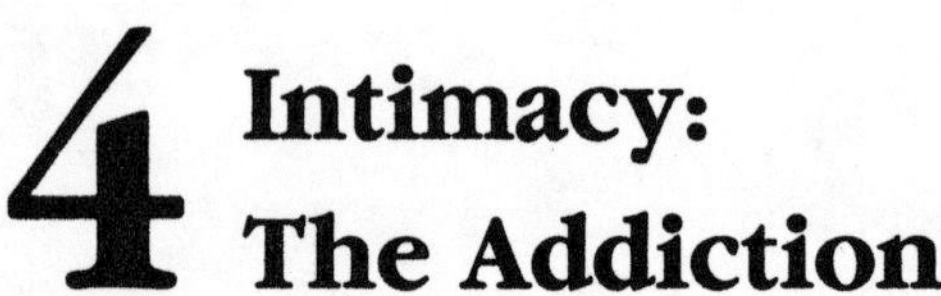

4 Intimacy: The Addiction

"Are we there yet?"

The question was asked—at least one thousand times (retrospect allows for some exaggeration)—on every trip my family made, whether it meant driving to Grandma's house or trekking across the country. And each time it was asked, the level of voice intensity rose and the impatience of my parents made itself more readily apparent by the brevity and staccato of the answer.

"No, we are not!"

That answer was always followed by a recommendation—or was it a plea to quiet us?—"Why don't you look out the window?"

Evidently, my parents failed to realize that we had been looking out the window and we were tired of that game. Whatever there was to be seen had been seen and had been incorporated into a game or a contest or a school project.

"Are we there yet?"

We all have a tendency to see our relationships in this same way. *Are we there yet?* we wonder. In the back of our minds there is the assumption that there is someplace to arrive—once and for all—where all questions are resolved, discomfort evaporated, confusion eliminated, and choices made easy.

It is the hope to solve our restlessness. Everyone knows this longing to be more than he/she is. The problem—as we detailed it in the first chapter—is that this restlessness is seldom acknowledged and embraced for what it is. Instead, this sense of incompleteness is assumed to be a physical or material need. It is no wonder we are drawn and compelled by some substance or external magic wand. As a result, we use goods and possessions, people, places, and experiences—via romance or sexual encounters or the creation of ecstasy—to fill the vacancy. Alan Watts noted aptly that as the "belief in the eternal within becomes impossible, men seek their ultimate happiness in the joys of time" (Lenters, p. 19).

It's a distorted perspective of success.

George Leonard, a sixty-three-year-old black belt in aikido, is blunt in his observations about our culture and our predicament: "We are in an impatient society, dedicated to the quick fix. . . . For ten years I've run an aikido school near San Francisco. I've had the striking experience of watching students show up the first day with excited eyes, only to drop out quickly, at an alarming rate. Only 1 or 2 percent might make it to black belt. Most of the casualties are young men who are mainly concerned with looking good. They are usually preoccupied with overnight progress, with getting ahead without the necessary long-term practice. . . . We've got to accept the fact that mastery . . . is a journey, not a destination" (*Esquire,* May 1987, p. 15).

Are we there yet?

That such pragmatism is at odds with ethical introspection, long-term commitment, and friendship for its own sake, is a reality taking its toll on our relational lives. Our cultural bias toward success (and arriving at the destination) encourages a pursuit of achievement (and performance) in the area of relationships. Boredom becomes the ultimate sin. Ordinary is an indictment. Consequently, we equate adventure—fullness of life, pleasure, intimacy, wholeness—with nonboredom. And our cultural language implies that adventure equals ecstasy.

There's something in all of us that wants to escape the difficult task of stopping and uncovering those tendencies (and counterfeits) that lead us to disease. Perhaps we are afraid to see ourselves as we are—incomplete and human. Or perhaps we are afraid to be accepted there, and to accept ourselves there. We want to move to closure—on to some destination that still seems to elude us.

But there is hope. And change begins here. Many of us read the last chapter and responded with as much confidence as we could muster, "Okay, I can relate. I understand that I prefer counterfeit intimacies as a way of closure. But now I will change." It's not so simple. Underneath all of the counterfeits is an addictive cycle. And with the cycle come the questions: What is it that we are running from? What is it that we are running toward? Of what are we afraid? And is will power really enough as an impetus to change?

Intimacy and the Addictive Culture

I come to this place in the book with my own history as the impetus to my desire for more understanding in the area of relationships and intimacy. I am an adult child of an alcoholic. The reality of that fact impacts who I am today, and how I make decisions—or, who and what owns me. While I am aware that not everyone can relate to being an adult child of an alcoholic, there are some principles of human behavior and decision-making that affect us all. The culture that creates excessive alcoholism cannot scapegoat the alcoholic (or drug addict) for all the relational ills of the day. The problem runs deep and affects us all. It is the reality of an addictive culture.

Recently, much has been written about addiction and the epidemic proportions in this country. (See bibliography in the back of this book.) We need to take advantage of this research and the insights provided, for it gives us some cognizance of the cultural dynamics that impact the decision-making and relationship dynamics in today's world. Whether we like it or not, we have all been shaped by an addictive culture. How that impacts us, the world in which we live, the choices we make, the relationships we build, our perception of intimacy, and the way we learn, listen, and change is for us to further explore in this book.

What do we mean when we talk about addiction? Or addictive culture—or addictive system—that world where more is never enough?

Addiction is caused by our need to escape. It is fueled by our need to avoid unhappiness. It is characterized by our need to alter our moods. Addiction is our immediate and inappropriate response to our restlessness. Sadly, too, it causes us to replace a healthy relationship with a toxic one.

We are a culture of immediate gratification. We are easily enslaved by the pleasure carrot—that which promises enhancement, or ecstasy, or fulfillment, or any new variation on the theme of fun. We are made all the more susceptible in a culture that isolates the self—as self-sufficient. And all the while we are indoctrinated with these dogmas by Madison Avenue—an industry itself built on immediate gratification, ecstasy, self-worth by consumerism, and the right to happiness—and so the cycle continues.

The result, argues Anne Wilson Schaef, is that our culture inculcates us all in a disease procedure she calls the "addictive process." It is a process that replaces reality with illusion and counterfeit, and that progressively leads us toward disease and death.

To fully understand this journey toward intimacy and the relational choices we make, we must grasp the reality that none of us is exempt from this addictive process. It is too true, that "all have fallen short," says William Lenters, "of the freedom we crave" (Lenters, p. 4). He goes on to explain that "the addiction experience is the human experience, not the monopoly of a boisterous or boozy 10 percent of the drinking population. We all weave our own behavior patterns and habitually repeat that which provides and secures relief and escape. We may all spell 'relief' in our own way, but we all spell it some way. The human project includes passing through the crucible of addiction. Because everyone seeks safety, salvation, purpose, and meaning, we are all vulnerable to the addictive process" (p. 4).

Like Adam and Eve, mesmerized by the forbidden fruit, we seem caught between wanting something that is good, and not knowing when or how to say no. Like the mosquito attracted to the bug light, which will eventually kill it, we too find ourselves attracted to behaviors, obsessions and preoccupations which will, if unabated, lead us to misery—and even death.

For clarification, we must note that not everyone is an addict (by definition, an individual diagnosed as one who cannot live without an outside stimulus)—a word that unfortunately can become a catch-word or cliché. All of us, with no exception, are affected by a system—a way of life, a way of thinking, a culture—that is addictive. To continue our own growth and healing, it is a dynamic we must not overlook. (Note: It is not within the context of this book to explore the specific questions and issues that determine individual addiction. It is important to the thesis of this book, however, that all of us are impacted by the addictive and compulsive nature of the culture in which we live. That is important because it allows us to explore the identity currents underneath our relational choices. Indeed, there are an increasing number of people who are "clinically addicted"—that is to say, their identity is dependent upon an object, or person, or chemical, or some form of acting out sexually, and they are literally no longer in control. I strongly recommend further reading in this area—either for you or a friend.)

Some suggestions:

Out of the Shadows by Patrick Carnes (on sexual addiction).

A Time to Heal by Timmon Cermak (on being an adult child of an alcoholic).

Women Who Love Too Much by Robin Norwood (on co-dependency and family systems).

The Freedom We Crave by William Lenters (on addictions to sex, alcohol, religion, work and food).

Co-dependence by Anne Wilson Schaef (on co-dependence and the addictive culture).

Escape from Intimacy by Anne Wilson Schaef (on addiction to romance).

Addiction is buying into a cycle that "takes care of" our wounded and inadequate identity. It is a way to run from our restlessness and incompleteness. It is necessary because we're afraid to risk the possibility that we may be okay, even though we are human and incomplete—with the range of sadness, or grief, or loneliness, or even anger and rage. Our survival mechanisms (including the counterfeit intimacies), in turn, only perpetuate a false self. To see this scenario as played out exclusively in an individual arena is to miss the bigger picture. In reality, our culture perpetuates individual addictions by continuing to inculcate us with a flawed and fallacious picture of the self. It is a picture that encourages self-reliance, that rewards rugged individualism, that equates self-worth with consumption, that sacrifices the long-term for the immediate, that exchanges "being good" for "feeling good," and that defines success "in terms of the outcome of free competition among individuals in an open market" (*Habits of the Heart,* p. 198). Our identity has been divorced from any sense of community and investment (apart from our self-serving investment in achievement and ladder climbing), commitment, self-sacrifice, mutuality, fidelity, attachment, and humanness.

Why this addictive susceptibility? Because this "false self" is built on a thinking disorder, or faulty belief system that fears nonacceptance or even abandonment. This thinking disorder sees our identity—both individual and corporate—as tied to performance and consumption. It is shame based. Shame is distinct from guilt and comes from equating one's identity with one's labels. There's an essential inferiority that's assumed. Believing its message, we blindly fall victim to its destructive cycle—and we seek relief by finding some place to be powerful. Inevitably, then, our real feelings are repressed. But we are learning that our subconscious is a powerful force, and must be reckoned with on this journey of self-discovery. What is repressed eventually owns us.

What is it we are hoping to "take care of"? That, of course, is the root question—a question only further distanced by making the issue of relationships strictly a behavioral or cognitive one. Let's look at the cycle diagramed on page 47.

To fully understand this cycle, we must remember that it is fueled by misconceptions about life and growth, misconceptions that we internalize. For example, "Life equals absence from pain," or "I will be happier without pain," or "I must not be okay, because I can't make the negative feeling go away." Because we may not see (or feel) these emotions behind our need to seek relief, we assume it is just a behavioral issue. We then believe that change is just a matter of finding a different (or better) behavior. This in turn, makes us assume that enough self-discipline or will power will help us make the right choice. All the while, we are still running from the original emotions (or pain, or sadness, or powerlessness, or shame) which we have never been given the permission to embrace—and own.

The addictive process is the human condition. To understand intimacy—and the relational choices we make, and the patterns we perpetuate, and the antenna we wear that attracts the most unlikely people—we must face this addictive process in ourselves. It's not a subject we can avoid.

Nor is it new.

In the New Testament, Paul shared his own ongoing struggle, as he lamented that "I do not understand what I do. For

ADDICTIVE BEHAVIOR CYCLE

Our Identity Core

PAIN
Feelings of anxiety, weakness, confusion, low self-esteem, vulnerability.

Note: Feelings may be triggered by events, or memories, or certain persons. They "trigger" in us a need for escape from some pain.

CHOOSE TO BE A VICTIM. I feel comfortable because the pain is familiar. This choice to run from the pain of vulnerability will repeat the familiar pain of the cycle.

I CHOOSE TO FACE MY ULTIMATE POWERLESSNESS, TO FACE RESPONSIBILITY. It is an uncomfortable choice because it is an unknown world.

Note: This choice is best carried out in a support structure (small group or the 12-step program).

PLACE OF CHOICE

Note: Not an issue of will power, but of taking responsibility.

WE SEEK THE SENSATION OF RELIEF THROUGH OBSESSIVE AND ADDICTIVE BEHAVIORS.

Note: Substance—alcohol, drugs, food
Process—work, romance, sex, ecstasy, dependent relationships or co-dependence (need to fix others).

WE HAVE A LETDOWN. We experience anxiety, shame, depression, and powerlessness.

Note: This reinforces our feelings of inadequacy and our need for escape and security.

WE EXPERIENCE RELIEF

Note: Here we feel safe and comfortable. For the sensation or person or behavior takes care of something (whatever it is we're running from).

THE EXPERIENCE OF RELIEF ENDS

OBSERVATIONS:

1. This cycle is fueled by our misconceptions about life and growth, i.e., "I will be happier without pain," or "life equals absence of pain," or "I must not be okay, because I can't make loneliness go away."
2. Most people are not aware of the feelings and identity issues behind the need to seek relief. Hence the issue is assumed to be a behavioral one, i.e., "It'll be better when I find the right person for me!"
3. Growth is not just an issue of self-discipline.
4. This cycle is a run from real emotions and fear of powerlessness.

what I want to do I do not do, but what I hate I do" (Romans 7:15, NIV). It is the reality of sin. We are creatures whose paradise is lost. At creation, humans were given the power that comes from freedom, the freedom to enjoy, the freedom to say no, the freedom to trust. What we did not understand was this: Our freedom was contingent and was based upon the reality that our identity was already intact, and we didn't need to prove anything to anyone with our choices (or even with our right behaviors, or our learned shame-based labels —"super parent," perfect child, class clown, model of respectability, etc.). We were free to live within the reality that there was nothing to prove, or earn, or pursue. We were okay without the need to run from our restlessness and incompleteness. We were free precisely because we were "owned" by someone—namely, our Creator.

All freedom is, in fact, contingent freedom. In other words, "I am free to make this choice, because I am no longer free to make another choice." That which owns me defines my freedom.

But we've all seen the forbidden fruit. Contingent freedom is not enough. We want "absolute freedom." We get it, if only for a short time. Unable to be loved and accepted even in our shame (or with our labels), we seek some release. We look for the intoxication from breathing what we assume to be pure air. Who says you can't have it all! Its enticing promise is the very air we breathe, somehow finding justifications—"maybe next year"; "I got cheated"; "it just wasn't my turn"; "she wasn't the right one"—for the reality that the promise is never fulfilled. We still hope that there is an external solution. "Are we there yet?" we wonder with the next friend, or mate, or house, or job advance, or raise, or child, or lover, or kiss—as if each is hiding a promise and a guarantee of relief and hope. Nor will it do to hope that our problems will be solved when we get our friends "fixed," living as if the culpability of all negative relationship issues can be attributed to them ("I have a relationship problem, let me tell you about him!" as one young woman phrased her dilemma; "If only she were more caring and understanding," said her friend), conveniently ignoring that she put up the antenna to attract the jerk in the first place. And believing that our hope for better relationships, and therefore a better life, is somehow externally referenced, we miss the point that intimacy is ultimately an identity issue.

Given what was said earlier, it is not surprising that this addictive cycle is only intensified in our culture. Each new generation is confronted with the dilemma of extricating itself from the tangled web woven by a society that places a premium on immediate gratification, that encourages the emulation of the "lifestyles of the rich and famous," that is energized by consumerism, and that sees the weekend as an escape from the week—as a model for all of life and relations. It is no wonder that we are a culture consumed by addictions. Alcohol, drugs, romance, success, sex, religion, the "American dream," are all variations on the same theme.

This leads us all to wonder: *What is it, exactly, that we are to do with this information?* Deny it? Blame? Self-pity? Despair? Apathy? Avoidance? Somehow, we want to see this information as interesting, but at best only corollary to our real world, and the world of our relational forays and fears. To see ourselves as somehow affected by, and even entwined in, the thinking disorder and faulty belief system of an addictive culture, is too incriminating, as if we are now the recipient of a sentence of doom.

The Need for Confession

As we pointed out earlier, no one said the journey toward intimacy—toward becoming real—would be easy. We are all like the Velveteen Rabbit. We don't particularly want to lose our whiskers, or get loose and shabby in the joints, if that is what it takes to be real.

However, we must keep returning to the fact that our healing—as individuals and as a nation—can only come with honesty. Healing and growth begin with the biblical concept of "confession." It literally means to take responsibility for oneself. It is to say, "I take responsibility for who I am now, for the choices I have made, and for the consequences of my choices." It is to say, "I will quit running from myself and from God." It is to say, "I no longer need to pretend that I am above being human. I am no longer all powerful." It is an inventory of healthy and hard introspection. It is a direct look at who or what owns us.

It is to slowly come out of hiding.

Unless our faulty illusions and relentless obsessions and addictions are identified, named, and brought to light for scrutiny, understanding, and a radical call for change and healing, we will be satisfied only to address the symptoms of our relational dis-ease. In other words, I can read all the books on meeting and mating the right one . . . but they will do me no good if I am still locked in a cycle that pursues a counterfeit intimacy.

Confession is a choice that can be made today—and must be made every day. It can be made alone, or in community. I recommend community—it may be a twelve-step group, or a small group in your church—because it offers encouragement and accountability. You may use your own words, or the words of fellow journeyers who have gone before. The first of the twelve steps is, "I admit that I am powerless over (whatever the addiction: alcohol, romance, ecstasy, sex, a sick relationship, co-dependency)—and that my life has become unmanageable." Or in the words of David, the psalmist, "I recognize my faults . . . Be merciful to me, O God, because of your constant love. Because of your great mercy wipe away my sins!" (Psalm 51:1–2, *Good News Bible*).

Confession, however, is an emotion-laden word. It conjures up images of self-loathing and endless recitation of sins, and drudgery. Perhaps our faulty perception of the word blocks our growth.

Maybe the comics can help. Charlie Brown sat in front of the psychiatrist booth. In the booth, of course, charging a nickel for her services, sat Lucy. She began waxing eloquent about life. "Life, Charlie Brown, is like a deck chair."

"Huh?" he responded.

"Some people put their deck chair on the front of the ship so they can see where they are going. Some put their deck chair on the rear of the ship so they can see where they have been. On the cruise ship of life, Charlie Brown, which direction is your deck chair facing?"

Said a meek Charlie Brown, "I haven't figured out how to get mine unfolded yet."

There's a little—perhaps a lot—of Charlie Brown in all of us. Maybe we need the permission to believe it.

It is the permission for confession. Coming out of hiding. Or what Sam Keen equates with "metanoia," or "repentance, reowning the shadow, (or) turning around." He goes on, "confession and repentance aren't feeling sorry for peccadillos, but seeing how we have been captive inside the machine of personality, a prisoner of ideologies, an automaton manipulated by defense mechanisms" (Keen, p. 146).

It is the permission to believe that our self—with its emotions, doubts, mysteries and potential—is user-friendly. It is not to be overcome, or feared, or tidied-up.

Our search for intimacy begins with the freedom to step back and face our unfolded deck chairs. We confront the counterfeits and idols to which we cling. We face the faulty "gods" that own us and the misleading tapes we play. We deal with the unhealthy patterns we repeat, the defense mechanisms we use for protection, and the identity checklists we have accumulated. Change begins with confession. It is the simplest step, and yet the most difficult to take. It means admitting that we are, in fact, powerless. Our counterfeits and idols do not save us. We are not above being human.

As a result, it is no longer necessary externally to project such evil (or shadow side) elements onto our relationships. "I have a relationship problem . . . let me tell you about them!" is the way our conversation may have begun. It is only when we no longer need to maintain this illusion of control that we can allow the first step to begin with us, that we're free to continue the journey.

What's the point? Intimacy begins with honesty and confession. Why does it matter? Because my—our—identity is at stake. Intimacy is not resolved by magic, or by being a victim of someone else. It begins with a firm and anchored identity. Can we find it behind the addictive process?

I believe the answer is yes. And it is the task to which we now must turn.

> "In order to be intimate, you need a self."
>
> *Anne Wilson Schaef*

> "It is the paradox of intimacy that it is a strength that can be acquired only through vulnerability; and vulnerability is possible only with the internal assurance of a firm identity."
>
> *James Marcia*

5 In Search of a Self

Intimacy begins with me. And with you. And with our willingness to take the first and ongoing step of honesty.

This is another way of saying that every intimacy issue is first and foremost an identity issue. Put another way, intimacy is the invitation for each one of us to come home—or, to be at home with himself or herself. And to be at home with God. It is an invitation—echoed in the invitation of the Skin Horse to the Velveteen Rabbit—to be real.

Intimacy is not just a matter of technique. There are no special edition Cliff's Notes on relationships or magic formulas to guarantee success. There are no one hundred and one best opening lines to win admirers. It's not just a matter of learning how to "pass the test," or "get it right."

The insidious temptation is still there for us to want to overcome life, or at least to rise above it. We are learning that the journey of intimacy, however, is the invitation to embrace life—incomplete, human, fragile, complex, mysterious, full, painful—as it is. It is a journey that begins with confession. And in the process, we learn to come out of hiding, and slowly embrace ourselves.

This invitation toward intimacy (and confession), we've discovered, is a double-edged sword. On the one hand, there's the hope of genuine relationship, the discovery of the authentic self, and the opportunity to embrace life as it is. There is the opportunity to experience and express very present and authentic feelings. There is the possibility of passion, wholeness, giving, vitality, investment, love, and joy.

On the other hand, there's the reality that we are all vulnerable. If intimacy begins with us, we're not sure how much we want to give away. When we embrace who we are, when we confess, we're not sure we trust what we see in this mirror of self-reflection. We're not sure we'll like what we see. We're not even sure we're willing to be loved—for being who we are. Can we be content with ourselves as human—and ordinary?

There's the rub. This road toward intimacy is essentially a journey of personal transparency. We wrestle with the uncomfortable reality that becoming real is a process which cannot be short-circuited by wizardry, or a knight in shining armor (or the princess with the flowing hair), or the addition of Relationship Skills 101. On the contrary, it is the ongoing process of learning how to let intimacy begin with me—and in me; it is finding clues to life in giving and receiving in a world where promises aren't guarantees, discovering peace in a world though I continually fall short of my predetermined expectation for *what will they think?* and *won't God be impressed!*; it is letting joy be my guide in a world where life is to be found in the discovery and not in the achieving . . . and maybe even the permission to believe that life is not an enemy to be defeated, but a gift to be received.

Asking the Wrong Questions

So what happens? We get easily sidetracked by continuing to ask the wrong questions. What are the five steps to get along with difficult people? We want to know. What are the four steps to attract a member of the opposite sex? Or to find a mate? What are the seven steps in understanding women? Or men? What are the three steps to conflict resolution?

Unfortunately, with such questions, we can too easily avoid the primary issue—namely: Who do we continue to take with us into these relationships in the first place? And how does this self impact our relationships?

It means that our journey begins at a level deeper than our behaviors. It means that beneath our decisions and choices and behaviors is a self, which for a variety of reasons and motivations makes relational choices and sends out relational signals—and becomes imprisoned by expectations, defense systems, addictions, counterfeits, and illusions. Freedom comes only when we receive the permission to embrace that self—the feelings, longings, needs—and come to understand why we make the choices that we do.

But what does the process of uncovering the self look like? And where do we begin?

Who or What Owns Me?

I saw an advertisement in a national magazine sponsored by the Humane Society. Of course, the purpose of the ad was to interest people, like you and me, in adopting homeless pets. The ad featured a full-page color picture of a puppy and kitten. As an emotional appeal, it accomplished its goal. I was immediately drawn to the picture. As cute as those orphans were, however, my attention focused on the sentence at the top of the page, which read: "It's who owns them that makes them important."

Then it was my face I saw displayed on center page. And

the leading sentence was a question—to me. "Who or what owns Terry?" And I began to wonder. *To whom, or to what, have I given my identity? And who is this self that I take with me into relationships? And why does it matter anyway? And why do I want to sidestep the issue of my identity by trying the latest relationship techniques?*

So intent are we upon solving the external circumstantial issues surrounding our relationships, most of us have never stopped to ask that essential question. But we cannot escape the fact that it is who or what "owns us" that determines the choices we make, the people we choose, the values we live by, the boundaries we make, and the priorities we set—and the antenna we use to attract others.

We began this journey by acknowledging that in each of us there is an underlying restlessness, the need to find meaning and a sense of belonging. And we said that this restlessness is a normal part of what it means to be human—to seek completeness. It is healthy. We also noted, however, that it is our tendency to see restlessness as a character flaw, an indictment against our ability to be in control. Somehow, we're convinced, we must be more than human! So we run. And we busy ourselves with the activities of tidying-up our cravings, of learning how to manage and respectfully arrange our confusing emotions, and of seeking reprieve (and a sense of power and control) through ecstasy and romance and sex. We want to find some way to be other than human. We want to be above boredom.

It's a catch 22. We want to be fully alive. To transcend our humanity. To see God face to face. And in the process, we erect counterfeit intimacies (idols) that we hope will solve the yearning.

How do we break this cycle—which is all a part of an addictive system? We ended the last chapter with an invitation to confession. It is the first step. We defined this first step of honesty as taking responsibility for who I am and where I am. It is owning my "belief systems," and facing my need to be powerful and "in control." It is owning my fear of ordinariness and powerlessness, my humanity. It is the step that allows me to look at my identity checklist.

Our Identity Checklist: The Labels We Wear

Who or what owns me? And what are the labels to which I am susceptible? Who or what forms the script—continuously repeated—on the tapes in my mind? Who or what provides the belief system about my identity and how it relates to the world?

This accumulation of an identity checklist begins subtly, sometimes imperceptibly. Perhaps even with a simple question: "What do you want to be when you grow up?" we were asked as a child. "What do you want to be when you grow up?"—you ask yourself the searching question all your life, as growing up always seems to be just ahead. "Be," of course, is translated to mean "do." And "do" is translated to mean "how are you going to make money?"

What's at stake here? The seeds of misleading tapes are planted. Now, we want to perform "in order to be recognized, acclaimed, welcomed, wanted. (We) crave to be part of something, part of a team, to share an arm across the shoulder, a wink across the room. (We) look to be greeted by openings made for (us), the cocktail party group opening its circle as (we) approach, a job opening, eyes opened wide, a pair of arms opened for (us)" (*The Male Predicament,* pp. 44–45).

There is no easy way to walk through this process. I wish there were, but then I didn't invent the process. I do know, however, that like any journey, it requires taking that first step. And whoever said that we needed to rush through the growth process anyway?

So let's look at some of the people, events and circumstances that make up the content of our checklists.

- *Family of origin*

It has only been in the last few years that I have realized the impact my family of origin has had on my identity, my relationships and the choices I make. That this would only be a recent acknowledgement is not surprising. As an adult child of an alcoholic, I perceived control—of my emotions, my environment, the reactions and behaviors of my family members—as a necessary virtue. Any implication that my childhood may not have been as perfect—as my story would go—was a sign to me of being out of control. To protect my need for control, I perpetuated a lie—a lie about me, and a lie about how my family has impacted who I am today. I told only the "good stories." Somehow I failed to realize that my memory had become very selective over the years. What was I hoping to protect? Or, of what was I afraid?

Freedom can come—freedom from repression and denial, and pretending, and running—only after we stand face to face with this part of our checklist.

The system in which I was raised is called (in the language of our day) a dysfunctional family.

What is a dysfunctional family? It is a family system where the needs and emotions necessary for the healthy development of children have been short-circuited or sabotaged. It is a family system where normal developmental needs are thwarted because of the energy needed to fight (by keeping composure, or maintaining the right image, or just trying to keep the family together) the "disease" in the family. Something—or someone (known as the identified patient)—occupies the family's energy and redefines normal family relations. The identified patient may be an alcoholic, a drug addict, a foodaholic, or a workaholic, a religionaholic, or even a narcissistic character disorder (for more information, see Alice Miller, *The Drama of the Gifted Child*). What's at stake here is not perfection, but the reality that the element of predictability for "normal" family life has been lost, violated or sacrificed. (Note: I have chosen not to make a clear delineation between an alcoholic home and a dysfunctional home. In a book dedicated specifically to the issues of alcoholism or chemical dependency or co-dependency such a distinction is helpful and necessary for more clarification.

Characteristics of Healthy Families	*Disruptions Caused by Parental Dysfunction*
1. Safety	Emotional unavailability of parent Loss of control in a parent
2. Open Communication (Conflict allowed and resolved)	Secrets kept to keep peace Facade of normality maintained Feelings hidden Conflict denied and ignored
3. Self-Care	"Scarcity" economy Feeling responsible for other people's problems Alcoholic's needs come first
4. Individualized Roles (or no rigid roles)	Family's needs dictate roles Roles become rigid, especially during times of stress
5. Continuity	Chaos Arbitrariness
6. Respect for Privacy (and sense of the self)	Parents become intrusive Secrets confused with privacy Unclear personal boundaries
7. Free to Change	Resists change
8. Free to Laugh	Is always serious
9. Focused Attention	Restricted range of emotions available

Because this book is not specifically about being an adult child of an alcoholic, I have chosen not to make the distinction. There is an addendum in the back listing books on the subject of being adult children of an alcoholic.)

Psychologists tell us that we are not born with self-esteem. Self-esteem—the need to belong and to be significant—is learned or developed in our family system. What's important here is not the need for a perfect system, with the elimination of flaws, but the reality that alcohol or some other identifiable dysfunction disrupts the ability to provide care, and the necessary environment for the development of healthy self-esteem.

What is the impact of a dysfunctional home? Here we can benefit from a comparison chart compiled by Dr. Timmon Cermak in his book, *A Time to Heal* (p. 56). (Some of this information was drawn from a list compiled by Dr. Wayne Kritsberg.) Although the list is written specifically about alcoholic homes, it is applicable to other dysfunctional settings as well.

Is this a convenient way to blame our parents for any problems that have plagued us? No. After all, we bought the tapes, and, for some reason, as adults, we continue to want to play them. Also, for some reason, as adults, we confuse our labels with our identity. It takes care of something. For reasons of fear or protection or confusion, most children of dysfunctional families have not been given the permission to stop and unearth those tapes. Nor have they been given the permission to feel the fullness of the emotions they bring, to diffuse their tyranny, and to make new choices.

What is the net result? As a child of a dysfunctional home, your identity is sacrificed at the altar of family peace. As a child in a dysfunctional family you learn to adapt by assuming a role—a role which allows you to deal (although inadequately) with your sense of rejection, or betrayal, or loss, or anger, or sadness. It becomes a necessary drama to protect the still undeveloped child. Apart from the role (this is our shame speaking), we feel bad, or worthless, or loved only very conditionally. And as children, it's the best option we have. So we play it out with all the gusto we can muster, grown-ups in ten-year-old bodies. *Where did our adolescence go?* we wonder as adults looking back. All the while, we don't really know that we're playing out a role, but we assume that we're doing what is necessary in order to have a family. Dr. Cermak reminds us that "these roles are almost universally found to some degree in all families. However, when alcohol or other illness disrupts these roles in a family, they become very rigid and emerge from the family's needs, rather than the child's" (Cermak, pp. 66–67). As a result, we become stuck in those roles as adults.

Some of us become the *hero* (or the *rescuer*).* This is the individual in the family system *who assumes the role of peace keeper,* the one who calms the seas. He smoothes the ruffled feathers and takes the role of keeping the family together. The "happiness" of "the other"—parent, brother or sister, spouse, etc.—is not only most important, it is somehow "my responsibility," reasons the hero. Somehow, my happiness is linked with my ability to make you happy—or keep you happy, or at least provide some semblance of security. This role is taken typically by the spouse, or the firstborn.

Then there's the *scapegoat* (or the *rebellious one*). From his or her point of view, bad love is better than no love, and for the sake of attention, he or she acts out in a variety of ways. Antisocial behavior, or even trouble with the law, high-risk behavior, disregard for authority—all are acted out with a sense of bravado and a tough exterior to protect the wounded child within. And often, the scapegoat refocuses the family's attention away from the identified patient to himself (or herself).

Or there's the *comic* (or *mascot*). This member of the family assumes the job of "court jester." The purpose is to relieve the tension through humor, silliness, and slapstick. This class clown of the home entertains the troops. And to that end, he or she is often goaded on by other family members to keep up the facade.

Then there's the *lost child* (or the *withdrawn* or *silent* one). This child for all intents and purposes disappears—not literally, but emotionally. The personality is almost shut down, perhaps for protection, and the child is characterized by ennui, lethargy, periods of depression. All the while, the child may survive through an active fantasy life.

Before we go on, there's an important disclaimer to be added. In an age of relational psycho-jargon, it can be

* For more information, read *Co-Dependence* by Anne Wilson Shaef. For comparison, Claudia Black refers to the roles as "the responsible one, the adjuster, the placater, and the acting-out child."

considered almost faddish to suffer from the latest disease, or relational malady. Being from a dysfunctional family can become such a fad, to such an extent that it can sometimes appear that all families must be dysfunctional. And to some degree they are. It is necessary for us, however, neither to downplay the seriousness of the pervasive and harmful nature of dysfunctional homes, nor to simply pass out labels of identification, as if our disease (or identity checklist) is some kind of name tag for membership in a club. Granted, naming a disease is vital for our healing. But it is necessary to go beyond that to the level of ownership. Our purpose is to unlock and open the doors of insight for the ongoing process of personal introspection, confession, personal responsibility, and healing (or the process of healthy choices). It is not as important that we say we've come from a dysfunctional home, as it is to identify protective roles that we have carried into adulthood—and to see how they seek a counterfeit intimacy.

- *The need to be respectable*

At one time or another, we have all believed that we are not loved (nor have received attention) for who we are, but for the role we are playing (or have played). With one eye on the task or the decision, and the other glancing over our shoulder, we ask the relentless question, "What will they think?"

The message is simple: Look good. Be compliant, well-mannered, respected, competent, efficient, conscientious, proper, appropriate, and nice. Somehow we've been conned into believing that our identity is something external to ourselves. At some point, we were handed a score card, and clutching it tightly to our chest, we have assumed that our identity would thereafter be judged on the basis of how well we performed. Without realizing it, we anxiously scan the crowd for the cards raised high—like score cards at a diving meet—to gauge our okayness.

Some years ago, Woody Allen made a movie called "Zelig," about a man who changed—physically—to fit his environment. His chameleon abilities allowed him to become black with black persons, heavy with heavy persons, etc. His identity was malleable by, and at the mercy of, its surroundings. To varying degrees, some of us feel caught by this same phenomenon.

Consequently, we focus our energy on what Paul Tournier calls "personages," or the development of masks (or roles, or false selves) in order to be loved or needed, as if we are on auto-pilot molded by the whims of public opinion. As a result, we are reduced to being a reactor in the game of life. It is what James Dittes calls the "frozen Joseph" syndrome, our being cast—or frozen—into an appropriate role. He describes the syndrome by relating an experience in grade school involving the invitation to be a part of the school nativity play. He was invited to play the part of Joseph. "What are my lines?" he asked. "You have none," he was told. "What do I do?" he asked. "You just stand there and make sure that Mary doesn't look bad," he was told. Frozen Joseph. "And I was good," Dittes remembers. He was congratulated by the adults for being such a good Joseph. But at what expense? For he realized that he never once had a real conversation with Mary or the child, or the shepherds.

I can relate to that story. The little Joseph in me grows up to become an adult Joseph, waiting for the acclamation of the audience. "You were such a marvelous Joseph!" becomes translated into "You have such a fine sense of humor," or "You have such a beautiful house," or "You are such an inspirational speaker," or "You're such a dynamic person." The consequence? I redouble my efforts in humor, home decoration, lecture delivery, and dynamism. I'm frozen, inhibited, narrow, restrained, paralyzed.

If we are owned by our need to be respectable, then stopping to look at our checklist is a frightening thought. For what if . . . ?

Alice Miller observes, "In analysis, the small and lonely child that is hidden behind his achievements wakes up and asks: 'What would have happened if I had appeared before you, bad, ugly, angry, jealous, lazy, dirty, smelly? Where would your love have been then? And I was all these things as well. Does this mean that it was not really me whom you loved, but only what I pretended to be? The well-behaved, reliable, empathic, understanding, and convenient child, who in face was never a child at all? What became of my childhood? Have I not been cheated out of it? I can never return to it. I can never make up for it. From the beginning I have been a little adult'" (*The Drama of the Gifted Child,* p.15).

The sadness is that the system works. But at what price? Well, "Henry was the good son, but it didn't come cheap" (*Zukerman Unbound,* p. 221).

- *The need to be successful*

We are all products of our culture. Somewhere along the way, many of us have swallowed, hook, line and sinker, that to be "somebody" you must be a "success." Although we were never given a written script detailing what this success would look like, we nevertheless busy ourselves with the task of being other than ordinary.

Granted, goal-setting and gaining achievements are a part of what it means to live in a goal-oriented, pragmatic, bottom-line culture. The problem is the way that script is internalized. Given our need to prove something to someone (we were going to have the best math whiz cards even if it killed us!), success was to be purchased only in exchange for our identity. It was no longer a matter of being good at what we did. We had to be the best, and not only the best, but spectacular and impressive and dramatic. Even awe-inspiring.

I can relate. When I gave a speech, it wasn't enough to be candid and open. I had to be relevant, as if the purpose were to be opportune and acceptable. It wasn't enough to be real. I had to be powerful.

So the success script unravels itself. Instead of real, and human, and authentic, one must be relevant and spectacular and powerful. It is no surprise that when Jesus was tempted in the desert by the devil, it was that same script—to be relevant and spectacular and powerful, all under the guise of being successful. It is a subtle, even insidious temptation. And it can own us. It is the message of Madison Avenue. It is the message of ecstasy.

- *Addictions*

As we discussed, an addiction is any substance, process, or person that alters our mood in order for us to escape some pain. It is our way to cope. A way out. An escape. But it doesn't work for very long. And an addiction owns us. It can range from alcohol to drugs, to sex, to the need for romance, to work, to food, to making money, to religion, to a particular relationship. In each case, however, the scenario is the same. It's our way of avoiding a deeper pain. The addiction takes care of something. It attempts to reshape reality. But like a subterranean river, it resurfaces in different places and in different forms.

We can miss the point if we see our addiction as an external issue—somehow overcome by will power alone. Somehow we believe that we could quit if we wanted to. Or we tell ourselves that if only we had more self-control, or more faith, we could stop. The result is a vicious cycle. Because we seem unable to quit, we feel worse about ourselves and are inclined only to continue our escape through our addiction.

- *The pain and the past*

"There was a dig at me in the cougar crack. What, I asked myself after the conversation, could I possibly do to heal the hurt, to wipe away the tears, to restore the innocence?

"Nothing, I replied to myself. Not a darn thing.

"No shooting star this Christmas" (Greeley, *Happy Are the Meek,* p. 22).

This passage from an Andrew Greeley novel will strike a chord in many of us. It is the reality that all too often we come face to face with a part of our past—the pain, the tears, the wound, the offense, the resentment, the damage, the ache, the grief, the memories, the scar-tissue—and it owns us.

I overheard one man talking about the trouble he's had getting people to forget his personal problems: "It's hard to bury your past when everybody's got a shovel." Too true. But perhaps it is we who freely hand them out. And perhaps we have some need to hang on to whatever it is that wounded us, like playing with the fire that burned us, or like replaying the video of a brokenness, hoping that the replay comes out right.

There's a story about two monks who were traveling through the countryside during the rainy season. Rounding a bend in the path, they found a muddy stream blocking their way. Beside it stood a lovely woman dressed in flowing robes. "Here," said one of the monks to the woman, "let me carry you across the water." And he picked her up and carried her across. Setting her down on the further bank, he went along in silence with his fellow monk to the abbey on the hill. Later that evening the other monk said suddenly, "I think you made an error, picking up that woman back on our journey today. You know we are not supposed to have anything to do with women, and you held one close to you! You should not have done that." "How strange," remarked the other, "I carried her only across the water. You are carrying her still" (*Zen Flesh, Zen Bones*, p. 18).

Part of our difficulty comes with the belief that to be rid of the past we must forget about it, as if healing comes only through amputation. Consequently, because we can never completely forget, we practice emotional amputation—or denial—as if it never happened. Somehow we forget that what we repress owns us. Is it possible to see our past not as an enemy to be defeated, but as a child to be embraced?

Am I Somebody Yet?

There's a poignant scene from the movie "Stand by Me," a story about the friendship of four adolescents during an eventful summer. One of the boys was named LaChance, and the story was told autobiographically from his perspective. His older brother, Denny, had been killed in an accident, and his family had never adjusted. Denny was worshiped by his father, loved dearly by his younger brother, and was set up as an unreal and unachievable standard.

In one scene, the young boy was in a local grocery buying some food for the hike that he and his friends had begun. The grocer asked, "Say, aren't you Denny LaChance's kid brother?"

"Yeah," he said, wondering what would come next.

"Boy, your brother was some football player! Remember that year he made all conference? He could really throw that ball. Say, do you play football?"

"No," was the timid reply.

"Then what do you do?"

Am I somebody yet? The search becomes addictive and obsessive. And we become externally referented. We become a false self. And, says Judith Viorst, "This false self is compliant. It has no agenda. It seems to be saying, 'I'll be what you want me to be.' Like a tree that has been espaliered so that spontaneous growth is forestalled, it conforms to a shape imposed upon it from outside. This shape is sometimes attractive, sometimes marvelously attractive, but it is unreal" (Viorst, *Necessary Losses,* p. 56).

The pursuit was illustrated by the main character in the Emmy-nominee film, "Verna: USO Girl." Sissy Spacek portrays a clumsy, tone-deaf song-and-dance girl hired by a USO troupe because no one else is available. Verna neither sings on key nor taps with the beat, but she is utterly convinced that her destiny is stardom. She is sure that when she dies thousands will attend her funeral. Their memories of her will make her immortal.

Verna does not become a star, but she does make a hit with a GI who falls in love with her. Though she returns his love, Verna decides she cannot disrupt her career to marry him. And so the show goes on.

Verna pushes herself to perform during battle when everyone else is too scared to move. She courageously faces the criticism of those who tell her to forsake her "talent" and run back to her man.

Finally, a land-mine halts her.

An Army Public Relations Officer hears about the first USO girl to die in action and decides her story might boost morale. So foreign dignitaries attend the funeral, and bands march behind her casket. No one, of course, knows her name.

Having rejected love in pursuit of success, she dies without either.

But she does have a big funeral.

A story about romance, or marriage? Hardly. It is a story about our willingness (and apparent need) to sacrifice who we are today, for who we think we should be. It's about our willingness to sacrifice what we have today for what we think we should have tomorrow. It concerns the sacrifice (in the words of the old fable) of the bone in our mouth, for the image of the bone reflected in the water.

There's another illustration that comes from the world of "Mr. Rogers' Neighborhood," where the puppets have a conversation with Lady Elaine (a puppet not so pretty).

"What would you like to be?" they asked.

"A princess," she responded.

"What will you do?"

"I'll wait for people to come tell me I'm beautiful."

"Then what?"

"I'll say thank you."

"Then what?"

"I'll wait for more people to come tell me I'm beautiful . . . ."

In the wisdom of Alfred E. Neuman, "Most people don't know what they want, but they're sure they haven't got it."

What is the result of our brokenness and our striving? A distorted picture of the self. A lonely and starved self. A loss of our own inner voice.

I've Got Bad News and Bad News

I know one thing for certain. Looking at this checklist feels like too much bad news. It certainly doesn't qualify as a fun time! There's something about this scenario that goes against the grain. There's something unappealing about subjecting ourselves to such bad news. And we're tempted. In fact, it has been the ongoing temptation of the book: to find someone who will relieve us of our dilemma with a solution. We look for pain removal, a magic wand. It is the pressure for the author (or preacher, or lecturer, or teacher) to be a "public relations man," emphasizing all the so-called positive traits, hoping that the negative ones are never discovered. He soothes the audience, "Don't worry, I'll rescue you from any anxiety you may be feeling. I'll give you the answer soon."

My answer? Don't give in yet. For it is in this bad news—the reality of our brokenness, our addictiveness, our codependence, our relentless pursuit of the idols of success and ecstasy—that we come face to face with that which we most fear: our nakedness. It is in this process of confession that we see our powerlessness, our vulnerability, and our aloneness. We are afraid to ask the question that John Bradshaw asks every one of his clients, "Will you love and accept yourself for that?" Or maybe we're afraid of the answer—and the fear that we don't really believe that we can be loved there. Can we? The truth is unbearable. So we opt for denial, or the return to our addictions, or unhealthy lifestyles or relationships, or exchange one counterfeit intimacy for another—because of our continued and contaminated belief (or delusion) that we cannot be loved for who we are now.

Fortunately, our checklist is not the last word on the subject. And it simply will not do to allow such bad news to be the cause of self-pity. As we stand facing our pile of unfolded deck chairs, we need to know that there is hope. To that hope we now turn.

"If there is ever to be a true healing and helping, a true sheltering and clothing for any of us, it is with our nakedness and helplessness that it has to start."

Frederick Buechner

6 Grace: The Permission to Be Loved

We are in search of a self. We look for a firm identity. That is our task. Without such boundaries, the alternative in relationships is to be swallowed up by someone else. It may be more comfortable, but it is impossible to be a victim of intimacy.

This search for an anchored identity, as we have discovered, does not take place in a vacuum. Unfortunately, this isn't a convenient classroom exercise. There are no multiple-choice tests to make it easier. It cannot be reduced to a true-false quiz in *Redbook.* On the contrary. This "self"—our self—is wonderfully rich, complex, unique, multi-strated, and sacred. It works itself out in the push and pull of daily relationships in a world where disappointment is a part of the price of admission. It is a self that finds itself entrenched in an addictive and a performance-oriented culture, susceptible to the insecurity of an identity that is too easily tied to what others think, and drawn by the allure of the gods of the culture—ecstasy, power, relevance—and the counterfeit intimacies they offer.

Even after our look at our checklists and labels (and perhaps especially after), we come to this search with the hope that we can learn the right answers to make our life organized and uncluttered once again. It is the hope that life is somehow manageable. If only we could find the key—the explanation, the solution—to the mystery.

We're reluctant to face the obvious fact: Life is not manageable.

You see, if "life management" has become our goal and concern, then control is of the utmost importance. Somehow, unmanageable connotes out of control—or worse yet, powerless. And we don't want to be out of control. After all, it would be un-American—a slap in John Wayne's face.

It's at this point that we want to run—again!—to short-circuit the process. This is where it begins to feel uncomfortable, which is understandable. Looking at our newly compiled identity checklists may be enlightening, but it is hardly pleasurable. It is no wonder we want someone or something to promise us we can avoid the discomfort that will come with such acknowledgments—associated with words like unmanageable, powerless, vulnerable, mystery, intimacy. "Is there another path?" we ask. All the while we are working to prop up, and soothe, and defend our battered ego.

"But we're not that bad," we insist. "It's not like I'm a true addict or anything," said one man in response to a seminar on this subject. "It's a lot smarter to focus on my positive traits," said another. "Why spend time focusing on all this 'negative'?"

"We're not that bad" is an appealing objection. But then, who's keeping score here? And since when is being "that bad" unlovable? And why are we afraid of the shadow anyway?

It's the annoying realization that healing (or health) comes only when we acknowledge that we're sick. Or, out of control (or have unfolded deck chairs)—by which we mean that we are not self-sufficient, or divine, or able to "control" all the variables in life. (When we refer to being out of control, we do not mean reckless or thoughtless.)

Our culture argues that such an exercise is an act of weakness. And we want to concur. We still believe that somehow it is wrong to give up control. Are you sure that we can't fix the problem with some good advice? Maybe all we need is an oil change. We certainly don't need an identity overhaul . . . do we?

To compensate (and keep control, or at least the illusion of control), we adopt—or inherit, or invent, or scheme, or construct—methods for "life management." It is our attempt to retain some level of self-sufficiency. We're not ready to give in just yet—not without a fight anyway. And our fear of powerlessness continues to motivate us to strive and fight for security—or comfort. Still believing in our self-sufficiency, and our capacity to overcome our brokenness, or restlessness, we become easy prey to the promises of the cultural counterfeits.

But let's take a closer look at some of the methods (or systems) we use to manage life, the choices we make with our identity checklists:

We can deny that there is a problem (or we can become religious about it, and "let go and let God").

This is always an option. I can assume that the identity checklist is completely irrelevant. In other words, it is only a problem because I have chosen to think about it as a problem. The solution? Don't think about it. It's a piece of advice packaged in a rainbow of clichés: "Think happy thoughts," "Don't let it bother you," "Just pray and read the Bible," "Turn it over to God," "If only you had more faith," or "Don't worry, be happy!"

Well, I don't know about you, but I've given many things to God, and he has given them right back to me. Was I given the wrong formula?

We were led to believe that our problems could be overcome with proper mind (or thought) management. It was a matter of will power. And we assumed that faith was simply a commodity to be used in barter with God in exchange for an easier and more carefree existence.

Label it however you wish. It is still repression. It is taking the oversized beach ball of my emotions and identity checklist and attempting to defy the odds by keeping it under water, where I hope it will be harmless. But we have failed to comprehend the power of repressed emotions, still not understanding that what we repress—in the end—owns us.

Consequently, and not surprisingly, the issues raise their ugly heads again and again, only this time in the form of projection ("It's all the fault of the devil, or the communists, or the liberals, or the school system, or the church, or the government, or men (or women!), or my 'ex' . . ."). Or we sermonize or moralize. (The best way to cover a lack of faith is to preach about it in others.) Or we rationalize ("It's not really as bad as people think, after all, there are some people much worse off than I . . ."). Or we point the finger ("Did you hear the latest about? . . ."). If all else fails, we lapse into depression and ulcers.

Like the same old story, it is a hope for some kind of self-sufficiency. We show our strength by keeping a stiff upper lip. "Don't cry." "Be a big boy." "You'll get over it." We earn our math whiz cards by not feeling, by being strong enough to pretend its not a problem. And predictably, when we engage in such denial, we are the last to see (or admit) it in ourselves.

We need to be reminded that a healthy identity is not one that is striving to be free—or above life's struggles by denial. It is one that is learning to live and serve under the best master.

We can attempt to get our act together, or "find" ourselves.

We can perform. And in so doing, we can be "in control." It's our way of defeating these demons in our identity. We can handle it on our own, thank you. We can learn to structure the externals of our life to look appropriate—or holy, or successful, or in control. We can generate self-worth. We can learn the cultural formula for "togetherness." Or we can Christianize the formula and seek to be "victorious." And yes, even at the art of confession, we can become a math whiz. We can be like the Pharisee who prayed, "I thank you Lord that I am not like the Publican."

In this option, we have made the choice to assume responsibility for our own "okayness"—for our own identity. We've learned the role, and have pulled ourselves up by our own bootstraps. Unfortunately, this only serves to intensify the dilemma. The result? We only exaggerate the cycle of performance and consumption.

Intimacy, then, becomes very difficult. It confronts our need to be in control, to be the caretakers of our own souls (for belonging and significance), to be self-sufficient, to be king on the mountain. When we spend our energy trying to "get our act together," we find that:

- We see life only as a problem to be solved. In the face of a dilemma, we simply seek the right formula. Self-help books and tapes, positive thinking lectures, Zen, therapy, church groups—all intended for the purpose of fixing whatever the problem may be.
- It is difficult to receive. We must take or give to be in control. I become very uneasy when faced with my own shadow side, because I have not yet learned how to trust, or to believe that I am worthy just for being who I am.
- We begin to sabotage relationships from the start. Getting too close is frightening, because it exposes our discomfort. We believe that if other people really see our dark side, they'll reject us. So to avoid rejection, we leave before we can be left.
- People become objects to be used for our advantage. Because we're afraid of vulnerability, relationships become the means to an end.
- We learn to hide our real or true feelings, because we must appear to those around us to have our act together. So

we don't take the risk. The result? We only give a part of ourselves.

In one of his novels Andrew Greeley tells about a novice nun reflecting on herself and her relationship with the Mother Superior. "Mother must think that my true self is pretty bad. I am a much worse sinner and a much more proud and sensual worldling than she knows. I must hide what I am for a while longer so that I can finally discipline my rebellious body and will to measure up to the standards of the community . . . I will confess to her in the summer if I don't change. I still have a little time, not much but a little. I must resolve to work harder, that's all. Until then I'll continue to hide. Maybe someday when we're both old religious . . . I can reveal my deception and we'll both laugh and agree that it was a holy hiding" *(Virgin and Martyr,* p. 162).

We become overly preoccupied with adequacy. If having one's act together is the goal, we need protection for survival. We are preoccupied with this mountain on which we must be king.

A recent comic strip illustrated the point. Two single men were sitting on a park bench. One—named John—sighted a beautiful woman on another bench. "Wow," he said, "she's something. I'd like to ask her for a date." He goes on, "Yea, why not? What have I got to lose?" And with that he stands up and begins to walk toward the other bench. His friend calls after him, "Only your self-esteem, your confidence, and your sense of masculinity." John returns to the bench, sits down, and says, "Thanks for reminding me."

I think we can all relate to John. It is the ongoing fear of what we need to protect. We fear inadequacy—not measuring up. We fear losing what we don't have. We fear not having or being enough. We fear being compared, and being found wanting.

We can maintain our identity by rescuing others.

Some books sell a lot of copies because they titillate. But some books sell a lot of copies because they strike a chord of need. One such book was *Women Who Love Too Much* by Robin Norwood. Too bad, but I wish it would have been called "people who love too much." The book talks about what has been referred to as co-dependency—the role of rescuing others.

It is a way of staying in control, by taking responsibility for others. It's been called co-dependence. It is another way of convincing ourselves that we are "together" (or worthy or needed). We have come to believe that our self-worth is contingent upon our ability to fix, or nurture, or protect someone else. Some have called it the role of the hero or the rescuer. We assume that it is our job—in fact, our duty—to make others okay. We are somehow responsible for their happiness.

We say that we just want to be a responsible person. Our worry, however, comes from needing to be perfect in our "taking responsibility." And too often, the role is played out without the conscious realization that it keeps us from facing our own anger and disappointment.

We can live our lives in retaliation.

Life is unfair! And we're tired of paying the price. The consequence? We are fueled by our need to get even. To balance the scales. What is the alternative in an unfair world? Bitterness, says this option. Don't get mad, get even, is the byline. If you love something let it go, and if it doesn't come back, hunt it down and kill it! That is our lifelong bumper sticker. And we enter all events and relationships with a grudge.

Life is guilty until proven innocent. And sometimes we continue to shoot ourselves in the foot to prove that we have a reason for our anger. We return to the scene of the crime, or recreate it in other ways, in order to fuel the fire that gives us our only reason to live.

Are We There Yet?

We only perpetuate the cycle by asking, "How do I get rid of these characteristics on my confusing checklist?" It's the wrong question. It assumes that we can manage life by sheer will power, or self-control. It also assumes that health happens only when life is nice and neat. And it assumes that our checklist is meant to be fixed.

The issue here, however, is not to "get rid of."

Rather, it is "How can I learn to face and accept me, regardless of what I find on the checklist?" Or, "How can I begin to heal (and grow and make healthy choices) so as not to become a prisoner of these characteristics?" Will I love and accept myself for even that checklist?

It is also not important that you or I perfectly identify which of the previous four options we may fit. It's not our purpose—as we said earlier—to simply hand out labels. Labels are important in naming the enemies and demons we face, but the issue is more complex than that. In fact, you may see yourself in all four of the methods (or systems) we described. I know that I do. What is important, then, is that we begin to see that all four options avoid the issue of need—and powerlessness.

All of the above choices with our checklists seek to stay in control. One by repression. Another by activism. Another by avoidance. Another by anger. And they are safe. They never force us to question our illusions. They keep us stuck.

This is an important nuance. I know that many people want to short-circuit the process by taking their newly discovered label, and go on with life, with a vow to work harder, or to overcome the dilemma. But as we've said, it is not just a matter of having the right answer, or generating enough will power. Our health comes with an ongoing willingness to see that we cannot manipulate life or relationships by being powerful and in control.

"Are we there yet?" It seems that the question still plagues us, as if we can heal (or recover in the case of an individual dealing with addictive issues) perfectly. It's a self-defeating thought. But life and relationships are not perfect. And there is pain—distress and tension—for a reason. Our emotions must be felt. To push them away is to jump back on the merry-go-round of performance and denial.

Is there another alternative? Is there a path of healing? Is there a place where the ambiguities of life do not need to be pushed away? Is there a place where our checklists are not just more bad news?

We can stop and be silent. We can listen to a new voice about our identity.

There's a story from the Gospel of Mark, about the bombardment of messages concerning our identity. In the story, Jesus is propositioned with the temptation to see his identity in terms of performance, and rescuing, and the need to be respectable. The voices are loud and clear, "Everybody's looking for you!" (Mark 1:32–36).

Translation: "Aren't you going to go and be what they expect you to be?" "Come on, Jesus, don't you want to be a better than average Messiah?" "What will people think, Jesus?" "Don't you want to be impressive, Jesus?" In response, Jesus turns out to be a public relations nightmare! His response: "No." Instead, he says by his behavior, I choose to stop. And to be silent. To find a place away from the other voices.

Why? Because change, growth, metanoia, fullness of life, wholeness, intimacy, and health can come only when we are face to face with this new voice. And what does this voice say? "I love you regardless of what you have done or failed to do. I love you regardless of what is on your checklist. I love you regardless of your math whiz cards. I love you for no good reason."

It is the voice of God.

And why silence? Because God does not compete with the noise of the culture. He speaks only in a still small voice. When we are still. When He has our attention.

Silence. It is the step necessary to break the tyranny of our temptation to be the self-sufficient caretaker and king. In stopping we can hear our true master. "Be still and know that I am God," the psalmist writes.

Although I am writing from my perspective as a Christian,

it's not my purpose at this point to convince or argue for the existence of the Judeo-Christian God. But I do know that unless we find a place to stop and break the tyranny of the idols and illusions we serve, we are confined to perpetual consumption and inadequacy. Besides, ultimately "the question is not whether we believe in Him, but whether He believes in us. And we have the absolute promise—the Flesh of His Son—that He does. God is the Faithful One" (James Carroll, *Prince of Peace,* p. 482). Or in the description of Corrine, a resident of Garrison Keillor's Lake Woebegon, "Corrine didn't believe in God, but there was still evidence to show that God believed in Corrine."

Stop. And Listen.

We are all falling. This hand's falling too—
all have this falling sickness none withstands.
And yet there's always One whose gentle hands
this universal falling can't fall through.

—*Author Unknown*

Honesty (or confession)—with our emotions, our counterfeits, our checklist—can only come where there is a foundation of total acceptance. Confession is relational. It is not just ego-archeology. It will not benefit us to prescribe fifty repetitions of "I think I can!" This is not an "interiority" contest, to see who can dig deepest and find the most prized kernel of worthiness.

Confession begins with a different assumption. To rephrase Descartes, "I was loved; therefore I am."

St. Teresa of Avila's definition of humility is applicable here: "to walk in the truth of who we are." "For me," says Susan Muto, "that means piercing through the illusion of total independence and admitting my ultimate need for God" (Muto, p. 78).

It means that we don't have to be all powerful. We can admit that we are powerless. Now, instead of puffing up our ego to cover our insecurities, we can now be honest about both our strengths and weaknesses. We have nothing to lose; we have gained everything. When we're in control, we have everything to lose. It means that I can accept me because I have been accepted.

The Permission to Be Powerless

I remember one of my first visits to a Benedictine monastery in the high desert of Southern California. It was a new experience for me, and I was somewhat uneasy about—and yet anticipating—what would take place. During the lunch, while I was in conversation with one of the monks (who has since become my spiritual director), I realized that there was something unusual about our dialogue. He never once asked what I did for a living, who I knew, where I'd been, or what I had accomplished. The message was simple, "We like you just the way you are, and we're glad you're here."

My response surprised me. I was very uncomfortable. "You can't do this to me," I wanted to shout. "You can't just like me! Wait until you get to know me or something." I was afraid. Afraid of being accepted. Afraid of being loved. Afraid of being "out of control." Afraid that I didn't have four Kings to play against his three Aces. Afraid that I didn't have a chance to impress him yet.

I realized how powerful my old patterns were. And how uncomfortable I was receiving love. And how uncomfortable I was with me.

The lesson is illumined through a parable called "Dandelions":

> A man who took great pride in his lawn
> found himself with a large crop of dandelions.
> He tried every method he knew
> to get rid of them. Still they plagued him.
>
> Finally he wrote the Department of Agriculture.
> He enumerated all the things he had tried

> and closed his letter with the question:
> "What shall I do now?"
>
> In due course the reply came: "We suggest
> you learn to love them."
>
> (Anthony de Mello, *The Song of the Bird,* p. 65)

Anthony de Mello continues with another illustration: "I too had a lawn I prided myself on and I too was plagued with dandelions that I fought with every means in my power. So learning to love them was no easy matter.

"I began by talking to them each day. Cordial. Friendly. They maintained a sullen silence. They were smarting from the war I had waged against them and were suspicious of my motives.

"But it wasn't long before they smiled back. And relaxed. Soon we were good friends.

"My lawn, of course, was ruined. But how attractive my garden became!" (Anthony de Mello, p. 66).

In the same way, my ability to be in control was lost forever, but oh how light my burden became. My need to be powerful was lost forever, but how welcome the gift of life became. My hard-fought mask of staying above the struggle of my identity and reputation was lost forever, but how freeing it was to give up the tension from living life as the great pretender.

In confession—and the acknowledgment of God's acceptance—I no longer need to bury my neediness, or emotions, or desires. I can, with St. Augustine, sigh that I am "weary at last," and give up on my battle to defend my reputation, my mountain—of which I am self-proclaimed king—and my need for absolute freedom. I can, with all those who have gone through the Twelve Step program of Alcoholics Anonymous, confess that I am "powerless." One friend observed that those who have come through such Anonymous programs are indeed the fortunate ones, for they are aware that their lives are built on the foundation of neediness. Life can now be a gift. I no longer need to take it, or earn it, or deserve it, or perform for it.

With that gift comes the permission to face our own hostility, fear, rage, disappointment, darkness, neediness, childhood, memories, resentment, anxiety, boredom, terror, helplessness, loneliness, confusion, and ambivalence. And to know that even there—and especially there—we are loved. We are okay, without needing to tidy up. Some psychologists speak of our need for "reparenting." It is our need and permission to give new and clear messages to the child within, the permission to let me love me.

It is no longer a journey which is intent on plumbing the depths of our potential. Nobody's keeping score. For in truth, we can dig deep—and come up with very little to show for how impressive we are. We can still be a prisoner of the illusion that we must stockpile trinkets, souvenirs, battle prizes of worth—things, relationships, achievements. But in solitude, we are free to be loved for no good reason.

I know, however, that when we read such a sentence, we feel a sense of confusion, or surprise, or frustration, or even a pang of guilt. It sounds too easy. Somehow we missed the point—and fall back on "if only we had more faith (or willpower)!", as if we can learn to feel good about ourselves simply by eliminating negative thoughts. We labor under the assumption that this first step is a magic pill, or that it is easy to do, or that it will catapult us to the end of our journey.

But the first step of faith is not belief. It is just listening. It is stopping to hear that if we are loved, we are free to fail. We can grow freely without being preoccupied with our usefulness, or our appropriateness, or what we can offer by way of service that may be payment in kind.

Self-discipline is no longer a system of life management principles, it is a lifestyle of confession, a lifestyle that is focused. Now that we know our identity is intact—we know who we belong to—discipline makes sense. It is no longer to prove a point. It is not a matter of more will power. It's an issue of stewardship—more like being a vessel.

When Jesus was taken before the High Priest, he was asked, "What do you have to say for yourself?" (or in the language of "Jesus Christ Superstar": "Prove to me that you're no fool, walk across my swimming pool.") Come on, Jesus, show us your math whiz cards!

Jesus was silent.

It was the wrong question.

And Jesus knew he didn't need to impress anybody.

Why? Because when you know who you are, you don't have to impress anyone. You don't have to perform for anyone. You don't have to cower. Or punish. Or use.

We need to remember that the process never ends. There will always be a pull toward denial, or rescuing, or needing to prove and perform. And a continued look at our identity checklist produces only a debilitating self-consciousness. Freedom can come only when we hear that we are loved by God as we are and not as we should be. That he loves us "beyond worthiness and unworthiness, beyond fidelity and infidelity; that He loves us in the morning sun and the evening rain without caution, regret, boundary, limit or breaking point; that no matter what we do, He can't stop loving us" (Brennan Manning, *The Wittenburg Door,* No. 93, Oct.-Nov. '86, p. 15).

Maybe we need to stop. Right now. And hear it.

Listen to this story from Brennan Manning. "A woman came to see a priest and she said, 'Would you come and pray with my daddy? He's dying of cancer and he wants to die at home.' The priest went to the house and, when he walked into the man's room, he saw the man lying on the bed with an empty chair beside the bed. The priest asked the man if someone had been visiting. The man replied, 'Oh, let me tell you about the chair. I've never told anyone this—not even my daughter. I hope you don't think I'm weird, but all of my life I have never known how to pray. I've read books on prayer, heard talks on prayer, but nothing ever worked. Then, a friend told me that prayer was like a conversation with Jesus. He suggested that I put a chair in front of me, imagine Jesus sitting in the chair, and talk to Him. Since that day, I've never had any difficulty praying. I hope you don't think I am off-the-wall.' The priest assured the man that there was nothing weird about praying to Jesus in a chair. The priest anointed the man and left. Two days later, the daughter called to say that her father had just died. The priest asked, 'Did he die peacefully?' She replied, 'I left him at 2:00 this afternoon. He had a smile on his face when I walked out the door. He even told me one of his corny jokes. When I returned at 3:30, he was dead. One curious thing, though—his head was resting not on the bed, but on an empty chair beside his bed.' To this man, Jesus was an intimate friend, and so he died with his friend. All changes, all growth, all improvements in the quality of our lives flow out of our vision of God. And when our vision of God is one of a God of relentless tenderness, we ultimately become tender ourselves" *(The Wittenburg Door,* No. 93, Oct.-Nov. '86, p. 17).

PART II

Tools for the Journey

Intimacy is not where we arrive. It is the direction we are going. It is not the destination. It is the journey. It is not a plateau, or a campground. It is a bridge to being fully alive.

We began with our restlessness. And we said that it is an invitation to become fully human. If, instead, we see it as an indictment, and attempt to eliminate it (as we all do), we easily succumb to one of the cultural counterfeits—all which promise magic and ecstasy and control and closure. To break this cycle (an ongoing process), we must begin with confession (honesty or coming out of hiding). Confession is not fun because it means looking at our checklists and labels (which are full of mixed messages). With irony, it is in this cycle of confession and affirmation, that we begin to learn and practice intimacy—vulnerability, self-acceptance, healthy choices, the process of becoming real.

Intimacy, then, is an aerobic activity. By its very definition, it takes time, practice, and energy. Time, practice, and energy. By its nature, it cannot be confined to, or completed in, a specific time period (say, a month or a year). In other words, it is a life-long process. Eugene Peterson once referred to Christianity as "grunt work." The analogy fits the journey of intimacy as well. Grunt work is the doing of all the little things (the daily, the ordinary, the mundane, the boring) that make the big things (esteem, respect, nurture, intimacy, worth, significance) possible.

Tim Hansel tells a story about a book he wrote on fathering. During the writing, he asked his two sons how they knew that Dad loved them. Tim assumed that they would respond by recalling stories of Disneyland vacations and Christmas-time gifts. They didn't. Instead, they paused, and then said, "We know you love us when you wrestle with us."

Wrestling. Grunt work. It is the awareness that in the middle of what seems so mundane, ordinary, even banal, is the seed for intimacy. So focused on Disneyland and Christmas, we miss moments of intimacy when they happen to us. Said one woman at a recent seminar, "One thing that bothers me about life, it is so daily!" Humorous, yes. But she's got a point.

And perhaps, that is what we dislike the most about the subject of intimacy.

Our capacity to live life "daily," to see all of life as a gift, is contingent on our belief that one's identity is already intact in the hands of a loving and faithful God. The journey is no longer an exercise in self-will, or will-power, or clever techniques, or positive thinking. We can begin the journey of risk and vulnerability and change and growth, because we know that we are loved, even with our dandelions and unfolded deck chairs.

It is not easy being accepted. So we have looked at the ways in which we guard ourselves against vulnerability—and the ways in which we may prefer to be victims or prisoners in the area of intimacy. When we are accepted, just for being us, we know we're no longer prisoners. It's difficult, especially when we know we must give up being a victim, when we accept that we are indeed free. There are choices that we can make for the health of our identity, and decisions that we can make which create change. There are environments we can nurture. What's the result? In the words of a familiar poem:

> "So you plant your own garden and decorate
> Your own soul, instead of waiting
> For someone to bring you flowers."

Two of my friends, Frog and Toad (from a series of books for children—including children in adult bodies—by Arnold Lobel) had a conversation about gardens. After seeing Frog's garden, Toad wanted one of his own and was given some seeds by Frog, and "soon" he was promised a garden. "How soon?" Toad wanted to know. In his impatience, he tried many ways—yelling commands, lighting candles, singing songs, reading poems, playing music—to speed up his garden (and alleviate the fear of his seeds), but to no avail. Frog offered his advice, "Leave them alone for a few days. Let the sun shine on them. Let the rain fall on them. Only then will you have a garden."

That's good advice for us.

In this section we will take a look at that "garden" and ask, "What does it look like—this garden suitable for healthy relationships?" What kind of soil is necessary for us, in order to nourish and cultivate intimacy? What are the environments that kindle intimacy? What are the essential ingredients for a healthy growth? And what are the choices we can make that will foster intimacy? And are there any "signs" of advice to guide the way?

"If your ego's basic existence is not identified with what you do, then you are free to play, to experiment, to take risks, to innovate."

Andrew Greeley

"Just to be is a blessing.
Just to live is holy."

Abraham Heschel

7 Permission to Invest: Permission to Be Human

You may be wondering . . . does our search for intimacy mean the eventual elimination of these loose ends of our humanity? Isn't the goal to finally get our act together? Is there a place that we can arrive, and prove that we have finally achieved or attained intimacy? And what does the destination look like anyway?

It is a difficult adjustment to let intimacy be the direction we are going, and not the place we arrive. To let it be the glasses through which we view life and not an object to possess. To let it be our ability to (continually, as on a journey) embrace our brokenness. With an anchored identity, we can see the journey as the permission to accept our humanness—including the full range of our emotions, our dandelions, our unfolded deck chairs, and our incompleteness. It is to be accepted, as we are.

The journey of intimacy is the unfolding of our humanness.

It is not a run from, but a run toward. That truth is the premise of this book. And this will mean a shift—in some cases, a radical shift—in the way we view life and relationships. It's as if we have been given the opportunity to look at ourselves, others, and the world through a new pair of glasses. These glasses allow us to see that life—including our humanness, our identity, with its assets and liabilities—is a mystery to be celebrated, and not a problem to be solved. What is at stake is not getting the right answers, or learning the right technique, or accumulating the right insights, or finding the right people to love, or even changing the people we love now. What's important is the reality that if we are loved (that we do, in fact, have worth and dignity not contingent upon math whiz cards), we have the permission—

- to celebrate life,
- to choose, and not just react,
- to receive and not just take,
- to invest—to be fully alive—and not just go through the motions,
- to walk in the truth of who we are, and not who we should be,
- to be human,
- to feel the whole range of our emotions,
- to no longer be just a spectator in the parade of life.

It is the difference between destination and journey. It is the difference between a Western approach to life, and an Eastern (or Zen) approach. The Western approach sees life as a destination—it's where you arrive, bottom-line pragmatics, turning a profit, public opinion, collecting the most toys, win at all costs. The Zen approach says that life "can never be forced; it can only be nurtured and encouraged. Recovery (or growth, or healing, or maturation, or development) means getting out of the driver's seat on occasion and accepting that some aspects of our lives can proceed quite well without our having to control them with our conscious minds" (Cermak, p. 27).

It means seeing life through new eyes.

And yet, our dilemma seems to persist. There is something unsettling and even unappealing about such an invitation.

There is something in all of us that views our humanity as a liability, to be overcome, or at least to be rendered manageable. The passions of our humanity—our need to take and to not be taken—are exchanged for a facade of decency. Weakness is seen as a cancer to be removed. In a world created according to "what others think" and "won't God be impressed," we slowly atrophy into our own world of predictability. Risk is avoided. "For what if we fail?" our internal bookkeeper reminds us. Security is preferred to growth. And if we do seek growth, we go about it with our well-worn guidelines for perfection and control. We rest content in the realization that our humanity has been made civil—even respectable—not realizing that the last flickers of life may be extinguished.

Now, of all things, we're told to believe that we are loved for no good reason. Our self-worth is not contingent upon who we know, or what we've done or failed to do. Our humanity can be celebrated. Intimacy is not where you arrive, but the direction you are going.

But what difference does it make? What are the practical implications? What does life—and intimacy—look like through "new glasses"? What does it mean that our identity is not contingent upon our successes and failures? What changes do, in fact, take place?

We have the permission to embrace our humanity—including the full range of our emotions, our woundedness, and even our failures.

It was a relief to me when I began to realize (ever so slowly) that I did not need to arrive somewhere before I could begin this journey of intimacy. Nor did I need to prove how far

I had traveled. The journey itself is enough. And it can begin today. The journey begins, and continues, with my ongoing celebration of what it means to be human.

In becoming fully and deeply human, says Gerald Vann, we engage in our primary "vocation" (*Moral Dilemmas,* p. 147). That may be. There's no better answer to the question, "What do you hope to be when you grow up?" than, "Fully human."

Here, of course, is the uniqueness of the message of the Christian gospel—the good news that God became "flesh" in order to redeem (to recover, preserve, salvage, return value, reclaim, set free) our humanness. God became real. Concrete. Tangible. Particular. Specific. With real emotions, desires, urges, and needs. It's the good news that also reveals our reluctance to see Christ as fully human. Perhaps this is why many of us want him removed immediately and forever off the cross, where he was hung, his flesh nailed, and murdered. It's too messy, too corporal, too tactile, too close to home. It's too difficult to remove ourselves by intellectualizing. The powerful and mysterious message of the liturgy of the eucharist (or the communion supper), is, in a way, beyond our comprehension and theological explanation. In it God exposes himself again in a wafer of bread and a chalice of wine. The awesome message of love is that God became flesh to make it sacred, to make us sacred, and to make the life we live sacred.

Grace is that way. It infuses life with sacredness. It announces its presence in the ordinariness of life. He is the God of the smelly stable, the Messiah of the carpenter's shed, of the saw and the wood shavings and dirty fingernails. He is the God of the wooden cross.

Grace infuses. Rather than being other worldly, or out of reach, or confined to the realm of spiritual insight, grace is the gift to help us take one day at a time, and keep us headed in the right direction. It is the gift that cannot be earned, or won, or accumulated, or deserved. "We can't possess it but, paradoxically, it possesses us. When we begin to let go, to release our brakes, we can taste its transcendence, even though we can't own it and, oftentimes, cannot fully understand it" (Hansel, *You Gotta Keep Dancin',* p. 108).

There are two impacts of such a gift. The first is that our liabilities are converted into assets. If there is no more need to keep score to prove our worth, we become whole people, "not on the basis of what we accumulate, but by getting rid of everything that is not really us, everything false and inauthentic" (Kushner, p. 150). Our humanness—with its secrets, needs, shortcomings, mysteries, contradictions, and desire to please—does not need to be overcome, or replaced by more admirable virtues. Our weaknesses do, in fact, become our strengths. Underneath the adult child of a dysfunctional family label is a heart full of tenderness and empathy.

The second impact of this gift of grace is the freedom to be thankful: for our humanity; for today. It is the relief from my need to approach life with a chip on my shoulder. Laboring under the "more is never enough" syndrome—"If only," I say, hurrying about in an attempt to accumulate, or fix something to make life finally worth living.

This thankfulness—seeing life with new glasses—is embodied in the following passage from the thoughts of the central character in a Philip Roth novel: "Ah, Clarissa, let me tell you, all that *is* pleases. The pond where we swim. Our apple orchard. The thunderstorms. The barbecue. The music playing. Talking in bed. Your grandmother's iced tea. Deliberating on which walk to take in the morning and which at dusk. Watching you lower your head to peel peaches and shuck corn. . . . Oh, nothing, really is what pleases. But what nothing!" (Philip Roth, *The Professor of Desire,* p. 198).

As I write this section, I am listening to Bach's "Mass in B Minor." I am absorbed in, and absorbed by, the music. It is compelling in its expanse, richness, and worship, its invitation to a full range of emotion. The music washes over me in waves of warmth, penetrating my barriers of composure and restraint and self-control. It evokes tears, feelings of passion, intensity, and an invitation to be a part of something bigger than myself. As I listen, I ache. Its beauty, its invitation to mystery and celebration, its exposure of my neediness haunt me. I ache because I cannot fully touch its power or its promise. And it requires me to stop, to listen, to embrace, and to be embraced. It is a reminder of the gift of grace—that in this moment, I am truly glad to be alive.

We have permission to be "tiny"; to see that there is no division between sacred and secular.

G. K. Chesterton tells of a young boy who was granted his choice of two wishes, to be huge, or tiny. As any small boy would choose, he chose huge. He was swayed by the appeal of being big and strong, in the same way that the young boy in me is swayed by the appeal of being potent, and virile, and helpful, and powerful. The outcome was predictable. In a few hours, the boy was bored. Because of his size, he was able to walk around the world in only a few steps. He scaled the highest mountain ranges in one step. Like a child one half hour after the Christmas presents have been opened, he asked, "What is there to do now?"

The young boy learned the lesson the hard way. Only "tiny" people can celebrate and enjoy life. They have nothing to prove, no score to settle, no one to impress. To tiny people, even the single flower growing from the side of a rocky hillside is an object of curiosity, beauty, and pleasure. Only tiny people can be truly humble people: unpretentious, approaching life not from power—and the need to defeat or dominate—but from respect. Only they are powerless, freed to receive.

Tiny people are free to begin to see God incognito in the everyday stuff of life (à la C.S. Lewis): the cry of a baby; the yellow and golden hues of a sunset; the damp and rich smell of the earth after a spring rain; the sensation of relief from a hot shower; the morning's first cup of coffee; tears during a good movie. Only they truly know the hug of a friend, the comfort of an enjoyable novel, the laughter among good friends. Only they can see the sunlight filtered through a bedroom window on a lazy Saturday morning, a smile across a crowded room and the memories of the smells of childhood—my grandfather's pipe, the burning of wood in the fireplace, bacon frying, homemade ice cream, lilacs in the spring, and Sunday pot roast.

In a comment about the work of American artist Georgia O'Keeffe, Alice Walker observes, "that she was not seduced away from the small, the common, the accessible, but instead made them huge, in her sight and in ours, so that we could not escape the visual beauty all around us by which we are so carelessly blessed" ("Elle," Nov. '87, p. 128).

The result? All living is—and therefore can be for us—a form of worship, because everything is touched and infected with holiness. There is no need to create artificial distinctions, as if this is sacred, and that is secular. Or, this is quality time, and that is ordinary time. The implication is that once ordinary life is out of the way, we can move on with quality life. And more is never enough. The truth is, "if you are in love with God you can paint a daffodil and it will be a holy picture, you can write a poem about trees or the sea and it will be a hymn. For through Christ our Lord, divine and human, all things are made holy" (Vann, *Moral Dilemmas,* p. 35).

The reward, suggests one thinker, is in living humanly itself. The pleasure and joy that come from good friendship, the enjoyment of satisfying food, a hearty laugh, the warmth of the sun, and the fragrance of a rose, will in themselves be the recompense for a life lived humanly. And there will be no temporary pleasure, whether from status, or possession, or ecstasy, that can replace this delight.

We have permission to make commitments and investments with ourselves and our lives.

There's an insidious notion in our culture that regardless of what we think, our identity is still contingent upon who has the most toys, or trinkets, or successes. Such a notion enslaves us to perpetual motion—always living life in the pursuit of our next goal to conquer, fueled by an ongoing regret over our failed pursuits.

At the 1988 Olympic Games in Calgary, Alberta, a story unfolded that exposed the persistence (and the fallacy) of such a mindset. Dan Jansen, an American speed skater—and one of the world's best—met disaster by falling in not one, but both events that he had entered. The first fall came on the day following the news of the death of his sister. It evoked in all of us who watched that day emotions of sympathy, disappointment, sadness, and compassion. And we wanted to cheer with all the more enthusiasm for the next race that Dan had entered. We all hoped for a Cinderella ending to this story of disappointment. After all, to come back from adversity is the American way. Then came the second spill. We sat in front of our televisions, stunned. How tragic! How unlucky! How unfair! To go all that way, and not be able to realize his goal, or his dream, or his potential. Somehow, life seemed less than it could (or should) have been.

In an image difficult to forget, the television cameras froze on Dan as he was being consoled by his girlfriend after the second fall. The newspapers all followed up with their version of the story, wondering how Dan would get on with life after having success pass him by. However, I was drawn to the comment of a sportswriter from Los Angeles who wrote, "Dan Jansen did not have a medal around his neck, but he did have her. He had someone who wanted to hold him tight, someone to say everything is OK, someone to tell him he's still the best, no matter where or how he finished at the Olympics" (*Los Angeles Times*, 2/19/88).

If Dan Jansen is a success, it is because he is invested in people. And people are invested in him. No amount of possessions or awards can alter that fact. "Loser's sour grapes," some will say. So be it. To see life and relationships as investments, however, allows us to see a distinction between perfection and completeness. The goal is not to eliminate failure. If life is the journey, then failure is a part of the process. Contrary to the advertisement of a popular light beer, we can't have it all. Nor is our lot in life determined simply by the luck of the draw. We were not meant to approach life like "ill-taught piano students" (à la Robert Capon), so intent on not making mistakes that we never really hear the music: afraid to risk; frozen by failure; afraid of what "they" think; afraid to commit; afraid to invest; holding out for something or someone better; afraid to feel fully.

From Antonine de Saint-Exupery we read that, "To be a man is, precisely, to be responsible." It is to be involved in the act of investing, or of entering into: the permission to invest with meaning; the freedom to be fully alive. Life is not what we have accumulated, but where—and with whom, and in whom—we have invested ourselves. It begins with today. If we are unable—even in a small way—to invest respect, or listening, or nurture in ourself and in the people who are in our lives today, what guarantee do we think we will receive, that such will occur when the "right people" walk into our lives in six months? In other words, this freedom doesn't grow in the abstract, or in the projected fantasy of a prince or princess. "It grows in a particular soil with particular people. Interior growth is only possible when we commit to ourselves and to others" (Jean Vanier, *Community and Growth,* p. 42).

It also means, then, that we are ultimately not a victim in the area of intimacy, waiting to react to the cards that life has dealt us. It is what Victor Frankl refers to as "responsibleness," where he says that it does not "really matter what we expected from life, but rather what life expected from us" (*Man's Search for Meaning,* p. 122). This is from a man who survived Auschwitz, a man who, to use our analogy, was definitely not dealt a good hand.

Intimacy is life through new glasses—receiving the permission to give ourselves away, or invest ourselves, slowly and gently, realizing that we don't need to impress anyone, by rescuing, or performing, or dominating, or manipulating, or accumulating.

There's an illustration that fits from Walker Percy's *Thanatos Syndrome,* where we find the main character,

Psychiatrist Tom More, reflecting on his life after two years in prison:

> Two years in the clink have taught me a thing or two.
>
> I don't have to be in a demonic hurry as I used to be.
>
> I don't have to plumb the depths of "modern man" as I used to think I had to. Nor worry about the "human condition" and suchlike. My scale is smaller.
>
> In prison I learned a certain detachment and cultivated a mild, low-grade curiosity. At one time I thought the world was going mad and that it was up to me to diagnose the madness and treat it. I became grandiose, even Faustian.
>
> Prison does wonders for megalomania. Instead of striking pacts with the Devil to save the world—yes, I was nuts—I spent two years driving a tractor pulling a gang mower over sunny fairways and at night chatting with my fellow con men and watching reruns of Barnaby Jones.
>
> Living a small life gave me leave to notice small things—like certain off-color spots in the St. Augustine grass which I correctly diagnosed as an early sign of chinch-bug infestation. Instead of saving the world, I saved the eighteen holes at Ft. Pelham and felt surprisingly good about it (Walker Percy, *The Thanatos Syndrome,* p. 67).

It might not be a bad idea to stop reading for awhile. There's no rule that says you have to finish the book today. Why not take a few minutes to stop? You can sit, listen to some music, or take a walk. Or smell a rose. Or call a friend. Or send a card. You can listen, and watch, and notice life—with new glasses. Maybe you can take some time to start a list of the people and things (in your life today) for which you are thankful. And then tell them so.

For they are the gifts of grace.

"By means of a diversion, a man may avoid his own company twenty-four hours a day."

Pascal

8 Solitude: Meeting a New Friend

"How are you with your alone time?"

That question gnawed at me, long after it was posed in response to a question I had asked about intimacy.

It sounds like a contradiction, doesn't it? Alone time, or solitude, as an essential component in the development of intimacy? Is solitude a necessary ingredient for this journey to healthy relationships?

Perhaps it is this very conflict that makes solitude essential. Our temptation is to see our relational dilemmas ("Go away . . . closer!") as resolvable via technique, or the right information, or an infusion of motivation for greater will power. We ar still laboring under the wish that the growth process can be externalized. The result is that aloneness (or solitude, time with our self) is then perceived as a bother, a cross to bear, or an obstacle to be overcome. Why? Because we're still afraid of coming face to face with ourselves—of finding our emotions and shadow side user-friendly. Such a response is predictable. As Pascal reminds us, "The sole cause of man's unhappiness is that he does not know how to stay quietly in his room." For, "in that room there is terror, but there is also terrible beauty" (Muto, p. 42).

In an earlier chapter we were reminded that intimacy is impossible without a self (or boundaries, or an anchored identity). And we learned that to nurture this self, we must regularly stop. It is only in stopping that we can begin to see underneath the film of "busyness" that covers us. Only then can we begin to peel away the layers of facade, and the paint coats of decency, and begin to chip away at the walls of fear and reactive protection that hide our true selves. It is for this very reason—uncovering the self—that stopping is not easy.

Solitude represents those times in our calendar when we purposely withdraw. Then we intentionally remove ourselves from the rush and hurry of life. We take time to sit face to face with the self (at least as much as we know of it). We come face to face with those times where our identity cannot be tied to what we do. Before we get too far in our discussion, however, let us be careful that our words do not imply inadequate images or create confusion. Solitude is not just aloneness, or being alone, as if we had nothing else planned—or our original plans fell through. Nor is it seclusion. Nor is it the sense of being or feeling lonely. With such a perception, some will want to avoid the subject because they already see solitude as unnecessary, or even cruel, or as a calculated attempt at isolation and protection. But such is not the case. While the elements of aloneness, or loneliness, or seclusion may be a part of solitude, what we are referring to here is intentional stopping—active quietism, if you will. Solitude needs to be a willful activity. This is not, then, a subject for us to deal with simply because we happen (at times beyond our control) to be its victim.

Let's Do Something!

Our initial temptation with any discussion about practical application is to "do something." It is no less true here. Give us three to five easy steps, O Professor! Our continual need for control seeks programmatic containment for life, for significance, for renewal, for intimacy, for purpose and identity. Solitude as a necessity? Okay, then let's *do* something!

A question was asked of a monk at St. Andrew's Priory:

"What exactly do you do?"

"We pray."

"Why? What do you accomplish with your prayers?"

"Is it not enough just to pray?"

Our Western mindset translates all of life into pragmatic components. All is measured by its potential value to our ability to produce or create or generate. We determine our existence by doing. It is not surprising that we do the same thing with the subject of solitude—or withdrawal of any kind for that matter. I find it curious that we live in a culture where after you have returned from a vacation (where you have gone to theoretically relax and do "nothing"), you are asked, "What did you do?" The same was asked of a group of persons who recently spent three days at a monastery for a personal renewal retreat. "Was the retreat of value (measured by 'what did you do')?" friends wanted to know. Or, the more insidious question, "Did you have fun?"

Intentionally stopping is a part of what the Judeo-Christian tradition has called sabbath. This is important, and our understanding of the necessity of solitude will benefit by our insights into the practice of sabbath, which has at its heart, intentional solitude. Sabbath—or day of rest—has been practiced by members of the Jewish faith for thousands of years. As a result, it has become a necessary element of the Christian faith as well. What's at stake here is not the resolution of the theological question as to which day of the week is truly the Sabbath (one which theologians over the centuries have not resolved), but the core issue, which is the necessity (yes, even the command) to stop regularly.

I conduct a seminar called "Slowing Down in a Hurry-up World." It's about our incessant need to define ourselves by our busyness and our accomplishments. Such hurriedness is a pattern that infects our relationships—and our understanding of intimacy. The seminar assumes that just as a rolling stone gathers no moss, so a busy and hurried person gathers no sense of spirituality or intimacy. In the same vein, I am convinced that on our journey toward intimacy we must pay the price of solitude (or the need for sabbath). Why? Because it is a necessary reminder that we are not omnipotent. We are not invincible. We are not ultimately responsible for the lives of those around us—even of those we love. Unless we learn to stop regularly, we haven't the slightest chance to meet our self, nor will we meet (and be able to draw meaning from) God, who "knows us best and loves us most."

Sabbath—What Is It?

Jewish theologian Abraham Heschel speaks of the necessity of the sanctification of time. For our culture—and the pagan culture at the time of ancient Judaism—the emphasis is upon things and space. It is an emphasis on possessing. Or accumulating. Or dominating. Or manipulating. And in our relentless pursuit ("the one with the toys wins"), we sacrifice time, and in the end, we sacrifice ourselves.

Sabbath as the sanctification (or redemption, or savoring, or restoration, or confirmation, or honoring, or preservation) of time is another way of saying that Sabbath is God's time. It is a time sanctified (set aside) for man to stop his worry, work, driving, performance, and preoccupation. It is a necessity to stop, a necessity taken from God's own choice to "rest." For what reason? Read the Genesis story. It is well known that God worked for six days. On the seventh day, he rested. He stopped. He withdrew. Why? Because he was tired? Because he was detached? No. He stopped to enjoy: to participate; to contemplate; to commune with; to relish; to savor.

We are reminded in this that our activism—and hurried busyness—only serves to short-circuit our capacity to be human, our capacity to relish, to enjoy, to invest, and to practice intimacy.

Sabbath means to quit. To stop. To take a break. In fact,

one author noted, there is nothing devout or holy or Christian in the word. The irony is that the implication is what we in America would call a "waste of time." Americans hear sabbath, and ask, why? But the plain and simple fact is that sabbath is not what you do, it is what you don't do. Sabbath, then, is the conscious choice to embrace solitude, to stop, to embrace the moment, to contemplate, to relish the gifts of life. The concept of sabbath is fundamental to our capacity to embrace intimacy. Or, to be more blunt, without a place to stop, we slowly sacrifice our humanity. As a result, we bury our capacity to receive and, therefore, to love. You can't have one without the other. You just can't.

Our necessity for a sabbath is reflected in a humorous Hasidic anecdote. It concerns a Jewish trader who so grossly overloaded the wagon on which he was to transport his merchandise that his horses could not pull it. He thought of lightening the load by taking off some of the merchandise, but later decided against doing so—because he felt that each item was indispensable to his career. Still, something had to go; so he took the wheels off his wagon (from *Holiness,* p. 77)! We do the same thing when we dispense with the practice of sabbath. It is a reflection of our avoidance behavior to avoid intimacy, with ourselves and God.

Instead, we *keep* the Sabbath by keeping all the rules. It becomes another obligation. We make it an issue of being good or bad. It becomes another place we can perform and keep score. The result? We feel like the Velveteen Rabbit. We want to be real . . . but, we're not sure we want to face the uncomfortable things in the process. Solitude (and sabbath) feels like one of those uncomfortable things.

One author says that sabbath is "quieting the internal noise." It is the time necessary for us to separate ourselves from the people who cling to us, and to separate ourselves from the routines and protective cycles to which we cling. In a commodity-dispensing and hectic world, we will always be susceptible to the heresy that we are what we do and what (and who) we consume.

Listen to Keith Clark: "If we are going to hear (God) knocking (and I will add, in turn, hear ourselves), we will have to make space amid the clutter and clatter of our lives" (*Make Space*, p. 11).

Elements of Stopping

Our first task? We need to unlearn our old understandings of sabbath. For example, sabbath does not equal a day off (or time off). A day off is a utilitarian invention. In other words, we reason, *It will make me work better.* Therefore, says our Western mindset, sabbath will "make me a better Christian," or "a better friend," or "a better worker." There's only one catch. We don't stop in order to "get better," as if society is one great beauty contest. Rather, we stop in order to embrace, and to be embraced, for who we are.

Nor is it the day in which we can do all the "little things" that couldn't get done last week. Nor is it always Sunday, for many have to work on Sunday, and it can be the craziest day in the week.

Okay, we concede. But how do we apply this? "Give us something to do!" Can you see the compelling pull to resolve the issue? I want to avoid the temptation of simply outlining an agenda for how to spend your sabbath time. But I can give you some principles, and they are choices we can make.

Sabbath is making space for God (or, giving in to God, or deciding not to play God, and giving the job back to him).

Before we get carried away with pictures of mysticism or monastic religious jumping jacks, let's stop and clarify what we mean by "making space." On the counter of a Wendy's restaurant, I saw this card the week before a Thanksgiving holiday: "Wendy's will be closed on Thanksgiving so that employees may spend time with their families." Sabbath is the sign around my neck that says, "I will be closed today, so that I can spend time with God, and with myself." It is a choice: to stop; to invite vulnerability.

Sabbath is our reminder that to be human is to be in union with God. It is coming home. It is what the twelve-step program calls "letting go" with your "Higher Power."

It is a conscious acknowledgment that our lives are given to relentless pursuit, to projected if onlys, to preoccupation with reputation and achievement, and to the fear of boredom. Sabbath is learning intimacy—with God, and consequently with ourselves—the hard way. In stopping—making space—we are choosing to give up our slavery to preoccupation, and in turn we are choosing to learn (ever so slowly) to give in to God's relentless and tender pursuit. It is hard, because it will mean confronting our fears about wasting time and being nonproductive, and about the terror of solitude. It is hard, because it means facing our sadness, rage, and fear. It is hard, because it means hearing that we are loved for no good reason. It is hard, because sabbath declares that our anchored and healthy self begins with God's Word about us and not our word about God, or even our word about ourselves. It is a place for grace in a nongrace world. It is the realization that intimacy begins with an image of our self in the hands of a loving Creator. It shows us that intimacy begins with powerlessness and an acknowledgment that we must receive. It means that we put ourselves in a place to be drawn to God by Jesus. It is a place where our math whiz cards are no longer necessary or relevant. If we do enter this "space" on our own merit, we remain anxious, undeserving, and restless. We soon realize that solitude can become isolation and terror if it is not built on a foundation of love.

Sabbath (or intentional solitude) then, isn't "interiority," Father Gregory Elmer told me. "Nor is it the continual plumbing of the vast empty warehouse of the ego—where we go to show films of how wonderful we are, which is okay until the bulb blows." In other words, solitude (or sabbath) is not a motivational trick or technique devised to make us feel better about ourselves. It is a necessity for intimacy precisely because (and only because) in our stopping we can once again allow our hurried and fragmented selves to be loved by a relentless and tender Creator. It is not an attempt to make people act or sound religious. It is an acknowledgment that we draw nourishment from the source of our identity. We may not, in fact, believe in this God. But—like Corrine—there is bountiful evidence to show that he continues to believe in us. Sabbath is stopping to hear that message of affirmation and grace.

Who is this unruffled cosmic suitor? We turn to Frederick Buechner: "God is the cosmic shepherd who gets more of a kick out of that one lost sheep once he finds it again than out of the ninety and nine who had the good sense not to get lost in the first place. God is the eccentric host who, when the country-club crowd all turn out to have other things more important to do than come live it up with him, goes out into the skid rows and soup kitchens and charity wards and brings home a freak show. The man with no legs who sells shoelaces at the corner. The old woman in the moth-eaten fur coat who makes her daily rounds of the garbage cans. The old wino with his pint in a brown paper bag. The pusher, the whore, the village idiot who stands at the blinker light waving his hand as the cars go by. They are seated at the damask-laid table in the great hall. The candles are lit and the champagne glasses filled. At a sign from the host, the musicians in their gallery strike up 'Amazing Grace.' If you have to explain it, don't bother" (*Telling the Truth,* p. 66).

Consequently, anything we "do" about solitude or sabbath is in response to grace. The choice to live sabbath is our regular reminder of that reality. And it means that if we make space to be with this God, we don't need to "clean up our act" to impress Him—with the right words, or flowery prayers, or religious feelings.

Some years ago, I was planning a twenty-four hour retreat. I had ambitious plans. I was hoping to accomplish a good deal of reading, journaling, and prayer. Over lunch I had a brief conversation with one of the monks and made plans to come back to talk with him over dinner. I returned to dinner defeated and chagrinned. At 1 p.m. I had briefly laid down, and to my surprise I didn't wake up until 6 p.m. I felt guilty and embarrassed. I knew that I had let everyone down—my friend, myself, and even God. (How grandiose we get!) I had intended on accomplishing so much, and in the end, I wasted my time. To which my friend responded, "And why is that so bad? It was waste to you only because you didn't accomplish your predetermined agenda. But maybe that wasn't God's agenda. Maybe he wanted to talk to you, and he knew he couldn't get your attention unless you stopped completely."

Learning to Be Useless

The permission to stop—and to be loved even in our stopping—is the permission to be "useless" before God. It is the permission to realize that God can only speak to one who has empty hands.

This is a good lesson. It is a reminder that our identity is not ultimately tied to our achievements, or occupation, or expertise. It is the realization that we are only free to be of use, when we can be useless before God. Sabbath, then, is necessary to remind us (regularly) that we are not God, that we are not king of the mountain, that we are not the manager (or rescuer) of life. We are loved just as we are. Therefore, we have no need to impress anyone.

The fact is simple. If we do not quit work—and make space—at least once a week, we take ourselves far too seriously. Some friends made the point with a coffee mug gift, with this inscription, "Who voted you Messiah today?"

Sabbath is the permission to listen.

Sabbath means listening in the same way that prayer is listening. I was once encouraged to take a pad of paper with a pencil, to lay it beside me, and wait to write what I thought God was telling me. It was meant to be an exercise in attentiveness, of learning to rest in relationship, of attunement. Because of my baggage, I did not perceive it as such. For me it became an exercise of merit, a surprise quiz for which I hadn't studied. I was afraid to leave my page empty, so at the end of twenty minutes, my notebook said, "Pick up dry cleaning. Call Tom. God . . . I'm supposed to listen to God . . . where's God anyway?" It felt like a rebuke, a failure. Under such tyranny, I had missed the point. I missed the reality that God is present, even in my worry, my doubt, my disbelief, and my laundry list, if only I simply receive him.

Another image comes to mind—one of hospitality. I picture my house, prepared for guests with attention to detail, the air, however, with an edge—a hovering need to please, and the inability to relax. I scurry about, refilling glasses, offering hors d'oeuvres, exchanging pleasantries. Entertainment replaces relationship. At the end of the day there's another picture. Norva (my wife) and I sit on the couch in our family room. Strains of Bach's "Magnificat" fill the room. Norva is reading a letter, and I am buried in a novel. There has not been any conversation for some time. But we know the other is there. And the very presence of the other is enough. Instead of rush, there is rest. Instead of preoccupation, stillness. The external pace stilled. The internal noise quieted. It is an analogy of sabbath—an invitation to listen. I am invited to rest with the Beloved, to invite the Beloved to rest, and to see the Beloved through new eyes.

Sabbath, then, is the permission to begin to see God incognito in the ordinary rhythm of life. Recently I heard a man retell a story about a group of people who had gone for a day-long hike through a wooded terrain on the East Coast. They concluded their day with a dinner. The central topic of conversation was the preoccupation with the speed and distance of the hike. "How far did we go?" some wondered. "How fast did we walk?" others asked. To which the man finally responded, "And what did you see on your trip?"

It's our tendency, even in reading this book. How much did we read? And when can we finish? And with our relationships we wonder, are we there yet? And with prayer, we ask, how much did we accomplish?

It was the noon-hour rush on a steamy July day and the two

men were pushing their way through the crowds in New York City's Time Square. They practically shouted as they tried to hear each other above the din. One man was a native New Yorker, the other was a Native American from Oklahoma.

The Indian stopped suddenly and said to his friend, "Listen! Can you hear the cricket?"

His friend was incredulous. "Are you kidding?" he laughed. "How could anyone hear a cricket in this bedlam!? You just think you heard it."

The Indian didn't argue. He just said, "Come over here and look." He walked over to a planter that was holding a large shrub, and pointed at the dead leaves in the bottom. To his amazement, the New Yorker saw a cricket.

"You must have an extraordinary pair of ears," he exclaimed.

"No better than yours. It just depends on what you are listening for. Watch this."

The Indian reached into his pocket and pulled out a handful of nickels, dimes and quarters. He then dropped them on the sidewalk. People everywhere stopped in their tracks and turned to look where the sound came from—some from as far as three blocks away!

"See what I mean?" he said. "It all depends on what you are listening for" (this story is recorded in Ben Patterson's, *The Grand Essentials,* p. 84–85).

The capacity to listen can only be developed in the person who learns to stop.

Solitude and Friendship

Solitude—in essence—becomes an invitation. It enlivens our senses to both what is external and internal to us. The act of making space, and listening, allows us (slowly) to embrace, or enjoy, or dwell with.

It is no wonder then, that solitude (as sabbath) is an integral part of developing friendship. Friendship is a sanctuary where usefulness is not a bargaining chip. It is a sanctuary where value need not be proved or earned. It is the freedom to be present—for no other reason than just to be present. It makes sense that the sign of health in a friendship is measured by the capacity of two friends to be together and quiet, comfortable with their silence. They are content to be in sanctuary from the world of politics and jockeying and one-upmanship.

The result is a picture of strength—a picture (from an Arnold Lobel story about Frog and Toad) of strength described as, "two friends, sitting along together."

Sabbath is intentional.

We cannot be "victims" of sabbath. It is not a practice that we begin when we have time. It is a choice. It is no wonder that in the Old Testament, it is commanded.

Primarily this is because it is not easy! Keith Clark, who in thinking about making space for God conjured up images of serene garden walks, reading, and speaking softly with others, underlines the difficulty. He says, "I don't remember such a day! I don't like gardening; I'm a poor reader; I usually talk loud. I'm usually to busy with things far removed from the natural and the humane. My life is filled with telephones, machines that don't work right, deadlines which have just passed without the job being finished, people who want to talk, cars that are a thousand miles past due for a tune-up, airplanes to catch or which haven't arrived on time, conventions to attend, interviews to conduct, talks or papers to be written, people to visit. Making space in the midst of all that is a trick. Space doesn't happen" (p. 31).

Making space—like all elements of intimacy—is an aerobic activity. It takes time, practice, and energy. Knowing that, I want to read this part of the book with the hope that solitude is optional. I want to avoid the reality that, by my nature, I seek behaviors of avoidance, and busyness, and denial. Making space and listening is difficult. This makes it all the more important that I practice sabbath.

Where does intentional sabbath begin? With a red pen and our calendar—and a red "X" that says, "I am closed here."

My theory about what you should do is not nearly as important as that you do it! Practice it. Stop. Try it. And if it doesn't "work" (as will be an invariable response), try it again next week. Our sanity depends upon it.

Sabbath is new priorities.

Singer Donna Summer recorded a new album after having taken over a year off. Afterward, she was asked about her career and future records, and she responded by talking about the necessity of a down time for health. Then she added, "But this culture is not into health. They're into tonnage."

Tonnage. It is the measuring stick of our culture. It infects our relationships. Why is solitude or sabbath essential in our understanding and capacity to receive intimacy? Because it is the price we must pay to fight against the pull to measure our identity and relationships by virtue of tonnage—quantity, performance, hurry, and ecstasy. What's at stake here is not a new program that one adds to one's life as the latest diet, but a necessary filter through which one must pass to embrace life.

That filter is sabbath: intentional stopping; intentional solitude; intentional listening; intentional receiving.

We find a great illustration in the life of Gandhi. It was well known that his spinning wheel was his center of gravity in life. It was the spinning wheel to which he returned almost daily. And it was that experience—that aerobic experience—that provided for Gandhi a necessary sense of equilibrium and balance. When he would return from the great public moments (events of adoration and even idolization) in his life, the "spinning-wheel experience" restored him to his proper sense of proportion, so that he was not falsely swelled with pride due to the cheers of the people. When he withdrew from the moments of encounter with kings and government leaders, he was not tempted to think of himself in some inflated fashion when he moved to the work of the wheel.

"The spinning wheel was always a reminder to Gandhi of who he was and what the practical things in life were all about. In engaging in this regular exercise, he was resisting all the forces of his public world that tried to distort who he knew himself to be" (Gordon MacDonald, *Ordering Your Private World,* p. 178).

It was a regular reinforcement—a regular intentional choice to stop and remember—that life and self-worth were not confined to the roles and expectations of the culture. Life is more than what we do.

We can learn from Gandhi, although I wish there were some easier piece of advice. I'd like some way to make the pill easier to swallow. But the implication is clear: Do you want to learn more about the journey of intimacy? Then practice stopping. Practice sabbath.

So where do we go from here? we ask. Sabbath seems to add more questions than it resolves. And, of course, I realize that I cannot resolve all the questions for you—as much as I'd like too. But you see, the Jewish leaders tried to do that, and they ended up with volumes of laws about what was, or was not allowed on the Sabbath. So my advice is a simple question: "Are there places on your calendar where you stop?" And when you stop—

- Does the time remind you of grace?
- Does it let you receive?
- Does it make you put aside you math whiz cards?
- Does it let you be quiet?
- Does it let you be centered?
- Does it remind you that you are not God?
- Does it let you break down the wall between sacred and secular?

Intimacy comes from the permission to stop, to be in our own company. It involves the presence and shadow of a tender God who is crazy enough to want to be our friend.

"Intimacy, then, is always difficult, and when it stops being difficult it stops being intimacy."

Andrew Greeley

"Very few of us are tough enough to be soft."

Merle Shain

9 Pain: Tough Enough to Be Soft

There's a moving scene from the movie, "The Unbearable Lightness of Being" (a story based on the book by Milan Kudera with the same title), that keeps coming back to me. Tomas and Teresa are married. They live on a farm in rural Czechoslovakia. The story has taken us through their lives in Prague, his career as a famous brain surgeon, their chance meeting, his notorious sexual forays, the Russian invasion of Czechoslovakia in the late '60s, their flight to Geneva, her return to Prague, his eventual pursuit of her, the oppressive Communist regime, his demotion to the job of window washer, and their move to the country. It is a story laced with passion, infidelity, shattered dreams, lost hope, lust, eroticism, fear, anger, jealousy, doubt, and renewed hope. Their dog, Karinin, who has been with them for their entire married life, is old and diseased, and she is about to be put to sleep. Teresa clutches her and says to Tomas:

"I love Karinin more than I love you. Maybe not more. But different. Or maybe bigger, but better. Because I can love her without the jealousy, the strings attached, without all the questions to measure, test, and probe, without the need to change or transform her."

Loving people hurts.

It has been said that the gift of life sometimes comes in surprising and unusual packages. It's too true. And the same can be said for intimacy. Like the proverbial bluebird of happiness, it is not always in the place where we expect it should be found.

But pain? As a necessity? As a component of intimacy? And why pain? It seems to be such an extreme.

Eldridge Cleaver voices our reluctance and genuine fear in a letter he writes from prison to a girl named Beverly Axelrod: "It is better to maintain shallow, superficial affairs. That way the scars are not too deep and no blood is hacked from the soul."

Don't Have Time for the Pain

It is no wonder that we give in to such advice. Our culture is built on the philosophy that prefers and regulates pain removal. In a world where weakness is despised, every effort is taken to avoid vulnerability. "Haven't got time for the pain," is an ad for a pain pill that lures us with its promise of a life above pain. All this is fueled by the secret hope that we are beyond mortality's claim—with its wrinkles, aches, broken hearts, broken bones and hair loss—on us. So we increase our defense spending—from Valium to Retin A—looking for a promise that life can be made a little easier. (Or at best, if life can't be made any easier, we can at least look good while we're growing old!)

But loving hurts.

This is hardly a popular message. The truth, whether we like it or not, is that intimacy is painful. When two persons touch, with emotions and self-worth exposed, misunderstanding, conflict, and hurt are inevitable.

It is a price of the human condition. To enter life fully is to risk being hurt. To invite intimacy is to be vulnerable. It is the sobering reminder we get from C. S. Lewis, that, "To love at all is to be vulnerable. Love anything, and your heart will certainly be wrung and possibly be broken. If you want to make sure of keeping it intact, you must give your heart to no one, not even to an animal. Wrap it carefully round with hobbies and little luxuries; avoid all entanglements; lock it up safe in the casket or coffin of your selfishness. But in that casket—safe, dark, motionless, airless—it will change. It will not be broken; it will become unbreakable, impenetrable, irredeemable. . . . The only place outside Heaven where you can be perfectly safe from all the dangers and perturbations of love is Hell" (C. S. Lewis, *The Four Loves*).

In other words, we cannot get away from the inevitability: a part of the process of discovering what we want is also coming face to face with what we don't want. As I write this, it happens to be a beautiful winter day, with sunshine, blue skies, and the fresh smell of the earth after a rainstorm. But I can celebrate such a day, knowing that it evokes delight only because it has been preceded by two days of dreariness: gray, damp, and cold. I enjoy my health because I know what it is like to be sick. I enjoy my sense of smell because I know what it is like to lose that sense. And I enjoy glimpses of intimacy (of being real with another) because I know what it is like to be rebuffed and rejected. This is not meant to be a motivational talk to begin to see the silver lining behind every cloud. But it is meant to point out that life is not as pain- and suffering-free as we want to envision—and perhaps, even remake—it.

You see, we've been inculcated with a cultural message that is accurately summed up in the words of a local bank ad: "Sign up today for our RISK-FREE account." That's it. That's what tempts us. And we want the same thing for all of life. Where can we go to sign up for risk-free relationships, risk-free involvement, risk-free social encounters, risk-free sex, risk-free parenting, risk-free aging, risk-free religious faith—risk-free life? We want a guarantee! Insurance! Can we sue life for malpractice?

So what's the point I'm trying to make? Do we somehow become more noble creatures when we see how pain-filled life can be? Or, do we need to somehow adopt a more pessimistic view of life in general—that, in the words of one popular philosophy, "Life sucks, then you die"?

The answer is *no.*

Love That's Guaranteed Is Not Love

The point here is that we're free to embrace life and live fully, only if we invest ourselves. Only then can we see that pain may be the price for such an investment. I know you are free to love me, only if you are free to leave me. You are free to say yes, only if you are free to say no. The reality (and the dilemma) is this: love that is guaranteed is not love.

Frankly, I don't like the odds here. And there's still something attractive and reassuring about the philosophy in a popular Country & Western song, which says that, "Hearts aren't made to break; they're made for love."

And we believe it. Or at least we want to believe it. We pay the price with at least one of three consequences.

1) *We keep running.* We can avoid getting too close by always moving—working, compulsive. We say that we have many "good friends." But what do we mean? Do we mean that they really know us? Or that we know them? Or is it that we have many connections—a good network? By calling them good friends can we still avoid the reality that we've not yet had to be vulnerable, or exposed?

One variation of this consequence is the co-dependent theme of which we spoke in earlier chapters. To keep running, we can take on the role of being a rescuer or a manager. We can exist to make others feel okay—to be the life of the party, or to be the listening ear, or the perfect parent, or the compliant spouse. While there is nothing wrong with listening and being spontaneous at parties, as a defense mechanism against looking at and feeling our own needs, emotions, and desires, it slowly paralyzes us. Our identity is tied to our capacity to be helpful. At least it gets us some attention. It isn't long before we begin to apply for the job of becoming everyone's messiah. "We'll fix it" is our motto, often needing to perpetuate a crisis to be needed. While rescuers save, managers boss. I protect myself by always being in charge. Because I'm afraid that my own life may be unmanageable, I easily find others around me whom I can manage.

It goes back to the issue of trust. Because of our fear, or woundedness, we're unable to trust. The issue of pain only reinforces our fear. At the same time, we're unable to see that our continued running (or staying in control) keeps the cycle going.

For some, it may even mean going to the extent of defining one's life by becoming a doormat for someone else, taking the role of being the ultimate victim. But here I need to stop and elaborate.

At a recent seminar, one woman came to me obviously distraught. She explained her situation, a ten-year marriage to a man who abused her emotionally. She was in great pain. And she said she came to the seminar for some advice and relief from that pain. But she was angry that my lecture implied the necessity of risk to realize love and intimacy. She told me that she had left her husband three times hoping he could change. In each case, after a few weeks she returned to him. But he did not change. And she was, she told me, tired of risking.

Her story is a good illustration of an important disclaimer. Being a doormat—or an ultimate victim co-dependent—for someone else is not a risking behavior. In fact, it is a security zone. The risking behavior, and ironically, the behavior that would precipitate the most pain, is to say, "No, you can't abuse me any more." Or, "No, this is not healthy for me, or you, anymore." The irony, of course, is that by being a victim, we can actually stay in control. Where would a bully be without his victim? Unfortunately, most victims remain isolated, and they are unable to find the support to make such a difficult—and healthy—choice. If you are in such a place, I hope that this book is an encouragement to you to seek out a support structure that you need.

It's not the purpose of this chapter to deal with the specific issue of abuse—either physical or emotional—in relationships. But it is important that we make note of the fact that staying involved in such a relationship is not a move toward intimacy. My recommendation to the woman above, and to any who find themselves in such a relationship (or series of relationships), is to find a support structure where personal needs can be nurtured, and a supportive environment can begin slowly to allow them to make truly risking and healthy choices.

2) *We are unable to commit.* This, of course, is nothing new. It is only exaggerated by a culture that promises more. Listen to comments of one single young adult: "I'm in a situation where I have to either commit to this guy or lose him, which I don't want to do. Yet I don't feel like getting married, either. I've finally found the right agency, the right job, and I get to meet lots of interesting men, and I occasionally choose to go out with one. Why give up all those opportunities for just one guy?" (*Esquire,* Oct. '85, p. 17).

This dilemma may come from the cultural pressure to wait for the perfect option, or it may go deeper, to our childhood fears of abandonment. In such a case, we may adopt the role of being the rejected one (or the rejecter). It's the "leave or be left" approach to life. Somebody's going to be left, so maybe we'd better be the one to do the leaving. In either choice, we keep one foot in the boat, and the other planted firmly on the dock, waiting to jump at the first notice that the boat may be sinking. Of course, in such a scenario, the boat always sinks. And we wonder why.

3) *We live life frozen and emotionally anesthetized.* For some reason, we find it easier to live as a rock and an island—a loner, isolated. Perhaps this posture is not calculated. But, "it is not worth breaking through the barriers of

the other's hostility and defensiveness." Besides, "we would only be jumped if we tried." So what's the result? "We want to be left alone; we want privacy; we want the lonely but safe little segment of isolation we have built for ourselves. Conquest and surrender are romantic dreams that have nothing to do with the harsh nature of the real world." In the end, "drifting is much easier than choosing. A life of response is easier than a life of responsibility . . . it is a life of noisy desperation" (Greeley, *Sexual Intimacy,* pp. 26, 132, 134).

That fact is, however, that "No one can escape the world's cruelty" (James Carroll). Of course, there's an insidious assumption that such acknowledgments will only encourage defeatism, and perhaps, even perpetual failure. But all of this hardly means we need to deduce that the world is absurd. As a result of a realistic look at the subject of pain—in the words of an English writer—are we to believe that, "(Life) is a tale / Told by an idiot, full of sound and fury, / Signifying nothing"? Or that somehow God has played a practical joke on us all? The only alternative? To be numb—the final defense against pain.

The Pain of Risk or the Pain of Regret

Can't we talk about something else, we wonder? There's a hope in all of us that we can avoid or cover up this flawed and painful side. The assumption is that the only other alternative is nihilism. But the issue here is not choosing rejection and pain. The issue is facing the reality of pain—the reality that there are two pains in life: the pain of risk or the pain of regret.

Risks must be taken, because the greatest hazard in life is to risk nothing. The person who risks nothing does nothing, has nothing, and is nothing. He may avoid suffering and sorrow, but he simply cannot learn, feel, change, grow, love—live. Chained by his certitudes, he is a slave. He has forfeited freedom.

Only a person who risks is free.

A part of me wants to write this chapter from a detached perspective, from a place of intellectual insight. But I cannot. At this point I come face to face with the empty spaces in my own soul from loves I've lost. A little over three years ago, Norva, my wife, and I adopted a new-born baby boy. We learned of Mychal's availability three months before his birth, and it was, to us, a seredipitous gift from God. We had been unable to have children to that point, and we were still uncertain about what our future would be as a family.

For three months we prepared to be parents. We were anxious and unsure, anticipating, all the while trying to downplay both our joy and the reality that what we were about to do was a risk. It's a catch-22. On the one hand, a part of you cries out to fully embrace another—to welcome your child and make a place for him. On the other hand, you're aware that there may be strings attached. Mychal was born February 24, a bright-eyed, healthy bundle of energy and joy. A pride. A hope. An investment. Not knowing what to expect in the case of an adoption, we, too, were surprised at the immediate bonding. He was our son.

Our initial days of parenting were not unlike most others', filled with second guesses, wonderment, confusion, bravado, hours spent staring to see what magic our child wonder would perform next, and happiness (not yet to be undone by sleeplessness). One month later, we received a telephone call—from a lawyer. The birth mother had changed her mind. In the state of California, we had little legal recourse. We were stunned.

How do you say goodbye? How do you give a part of yourself away? How do you say, "It was a nice try, sorry it didn't work out"? In the years since, a variety of arguments have been raised to "explain" the tragedy, i.e., God's will ("He had a better place in store for Mychal," or, "God has a better plan for you right around the corner"), to subconscious sabotage ("There was some subconscious reason you did not really want a child"), to a cosmic education plan just for us ("There's a lesson to be learned in this"; "What's God trying to teach you?"). This book, however, is not a forum to decide the reasons. Nor is life such a forum, for that matter, contrary to the well wishing of Job's friends. Regardless of any truth that may be lodged in any of the explanations, it was enough to know that losing Mychal hurt. Our pain was acute and intense and dark, and at times, even addictive. It was another reminder of incompleteness and impotence. And it brought up all the old childhood fears of rejection and abandonment.

Besides, I didn't care about learning any lessons, or becoming a better person, or being an example for others. Nor did I really want to feel. I wanted to withdraw. I wanted life to be fair.

But life wasn't fair. And loving hurts.

From his book, *When All You've Always Wanted Isn't Enough,* Harold Kushner writes, seemingly aimed at me, "More than that, I believed that it was supposed to hurt. In the same way that dead cells, our hair and fingernails, feel no pain when they are cut but living cells bleed and hurt, so I believe that spiritually dead souls can be cut into, separated from other souls, and not feel pain. But living, sensitive souls are easily hurt" (Kushner, p. 89).

Kushner goes on to talk about becoming less human by practicing detachment. I agree. It's not a matter of enjoying or seeking pain (which is a sickness), but of accepting that protection from the pain of life which carries such a high price. If we teach ourselves not to care, by quarantining our emotions, the loss is eventually fatal. Sure, we being to feel no pain. But in the same way, we feel no joy, no hope, no love. The result? We become skilled at living life in a narrow emotional range, trading our desire for any experience of zeal, or joy, or elation, for some kind of guarantee that will ward off tragedy and loss and need and pain.

Tough Enough to Be Soft

How does all this translate into daily living? How is it made practical? I can think of three reminders.

Pain is not an enemy to our ability to be intimate.

In other words, we do not need to be afraid of pain.

"'Man is born broken,' Eugene O'Neill wrote in *The Great God Brown.* 'He lives by mending. The grace of God is glue!' Which is a nice way of saying that living is the healing. Vulnerability is not a weakness. It's a strength. Very few of us are tough enough to be soft" (Merle Shain, *When Lovers Are Friends,* p. 16).

It means that we do not need to spend so much of our emotional energy constructing barriers against our times of weakness. We can slowly learn to embrace our powerlessness (or our dandelions, or our unfolded deck chairs), not only as a given, but as a gift. We don't need to keep score—or prove how strong and resilient we are. Nor do we do an end run around our feelings with a paragraph of theologizing or intellectualizing. Or derive some value from pats on the back by being a good martyr.

It means that we can, in fact, be tough enough to be soft.

A recent eulogy caught my eye. It concerned a priest who lived a difficult life, full of ups and downs. It said simply, "He was a broken old man. But he sure knew how to love people." It reminded me of a line from the song, "The Rose": "It's the heart afraid of breaking that never learns to dance." Well, I'm convinced that this old priest learned to dance. He didn't run from life or the pain it brought. He didn't roll over and quit when life caved in on him. He didn't carry a grudge. And he didn't pretend, with some self-righteousness, that he had some inside track with God, and therefore a secret resolve in the area of pain and suffering.

He knew—and practiced—that you can't walk through life with a full suit of armor that will keep life from getting the best of you. To be authentic means to slowly remove some of the protective layers to invite more of life in.

This old priest knew that "trust in life does not mean trusting that life will always be good or that it will be free of grief and pain. It means trusting that somewhere inside yourself you can find the strength to go forth and meet what comes and, even if you meet betrayal and disappointment along the way, go forth again the very next day" (Shain, *Hearts,* p. 65).

He knew that life is the ongoing process of losing and letting go. Losses are necessary. We will have to give up protecting our reputations in order to love real people. We will have to give up our need for control to receive any gift of tenderness or kindness. We will have to give up our need for life to be fair, to receive or give any vulnerability. We will have to give up our need to get even, to move on from a painful past. Put simply, life is not a contest to win. It is a mystery to be celebrated—a dance to be relished. And it must be fully embraced. Knowing that, we don't need to run from the pain and discomfort that come from risking.

We can be thankful for our pain.

Granted, we most certainly may not enjoy pain, nor would we wish it upon ourselves. We will not seek it out or create it. But here we are confronted with something fundamental about the human heart: love and pain arise from the same chamber. It is an empty space capable of embracing and cherishing both presence and absence. Such a realization leads Frederick Buechner to say that, "If by some magic you could eliminate the pain you are caused by the pain of someone you love, I for one cannot imagine working such magic because the pain is so much a part of the love that the love would be vastly diminished, unrecognizable, without it" (*Now and Then,* Buechner).

The irony is that only in absence is one's presence assured. In continual presence, one easily fades away.

There's a poignant scene toward the end of the movie, "Children of a Lesser God." It is the story of a man who takes a job as a teacher at a school for deaf children, and falls in love with a woman who had graduated from the school and continues to work there as a janitor. He hopes to teach her to talk. She is antagonistic and hostile. The movie takes us through their tempestuous teacher-student relationship, their developing romance, their passionate and intense and demanding relationship, their eventual breakup and reunion. "What have you learned?" he asked, in sign language. To which she replied, slowly and deliberately with her hands and eyes, "I learned that I could hurt, and not blow away."

In other words, pain is inevitable. Misery is the option.

We can begin to own our brokenness.

What's important here—and this we must reinforce—is not our attempt to resolve the issue of pain by advancing several moral lessons. What's important is the permission to believe that we no longer need to pretend we are invulnerable from the shipwrecks of life. We are not above it all. We can be human. We can truly be tough enough to be soft.

Morris West's novel, *Shoes of the Fisherman,* is about a man named Kiril who before he became Pope, had spent much of his adult life in prison. The effect of suffering on his life was evident in his approach to people and in the way he resolved moral dilemmas. After he was considered to be lenient in a case, two cardinals discussed their reactions:

"What did His Holiness have to say about that?"

"He has a soft heart. . . . The danger is that it may be too soft for the good of the Church."

"He has suffered more than we. Perhaps he has more right to trust his heart than we have" (West, p.112).

Secretly, there's a part of us that wants to be remembered for all that we have accomplished, or achieved, or attained. But the truth is that our success or fulfillment will have little to do with our productivity, or our cleverness, or our leadership qualities. This is because grace doesn't quit on us. If we let it, it may start to make our hearts soft. If we're honest, as we see the accumulation of external success in our lives, we're also painfully reminded of our own continued selfishness, our propensity toward self-sabotage, the imperfect connections in all our relationships, the capacity to hurt and be hurt. Our tendency is to cover up this human self with a firmer resolve to work harder, or to accomplish more—to cover up insecurity, weakness, and questions with a more together exterior. It's nothing a little will power and two aspirin can't take care of, we tell ourselves.

Then we read the story of the apostle Paul, and how he says that it is, "when I am weak that I am strong" (2 Cor. 12:7–10). Or we discover the story of "soft-hearted" Kiril. It is what Henri Nowen means when he says that we are all called to be wounded healers. Perhaps it is what Victor Frankl means when he talks about meaning coming in the midst of meaningless suffering.

The verses from the apostle Paul are difficult to hear for several reasons: perhaps because it is difficult to be human—and weak and mortal—and still believe that we're okay. Our tendency is to cover up that part of ourselves. Perhaps it is because it is difficult for us to receive. Or it is difficult to sacrifice our current measurement of success. Whatever the reasons, I know now that I want the permission to feel, and not to run from those feelings. I want the permission to know that life and loving people hurts, but that it doesn't ultimately cripple. We do heal. We can forge—out of struggle and pain—a heart that's soft enough to receive, and gently risk again.

> "Let him who cannot be alone beware of community . . . let him who is not in community beware of being alone."
>
> (Bonhoeffer, *Life Together,* p. 77)

10 Friendship, Community, and Liturgy

There's a story from church history about a monk who experienced regular and fervid temptations by the devil. He felt burdened by this oppression, but said nothing to anyone, and continued to fight it alone. Though plagued by doubt and darkness, he believed he could manage this battle on his own strength. This went on for some time, and he was not able to make any progress. In fact, he only continued to regress. Yet his pride continued to bet on his willpower.

It was only after great duress that he finally shared his ongoing struggle with a friend in the monastic community, confessed his weakness—and need for help. At that point, the devil was rendered powerless. Though the temptations did not completely disappear, they became less oppressive. Why? Because the Devil is able to have power only over those who assume that they are self-sufficient. But to those who discover—by owning and confessing—their poverty, weakness and neediness, the Devil cannot stand.

The moral of the story? That strength comes in the form of confession and community. It is not a new theme. No one is an island.

But, like the chapters that have preceded (on thankfulness, solitude and pain) we assume these ingredients for the journey of intimacy are at best, optional. The temptation is no different here. Still within earshot of our childhood memories of "Hi Ho Silver, away!", we want to believe that life is a proposition to be mastered by self-reliance, ingenuity and intestinal fortitude. Armed with this cultural philosophy of self-sufficiency, we approach life and relationships as win-lose scenarios. And we remain conquerors and competitors, not lovers and friends.

The implication, however, is inescapable. There's something about community—a place that counters our pull toward self-sufficiency—that is essential to our well-being. In the New Testament, there's a text which talks about the radical nature of this concept. "'Who is my mother? Who are my brothers?'; and pointing to the disciples, Jesus said, 'Here are my mother and brothers'" (Matt. 12:48–50 NEB). It's a curious and unexpected statement. Jesus wants us to experience fullness of life—and the text implies that such cannot be found in isolation, not in the narrow confines of our genetic family. Jesus is hardly implying that our genetic families are not important. (We can always make the text say something that it is not saying.) Rather, he is redefining the "Kingdom of God." And he is saying that the Kingdom is essentially relationships—not just orthodoxy. In his surprise declaration, Jesus is redirecting us to understand the significance of the new family relationships created by his life, death and resurrection.

"We're on this journey together," he is saying to all who will listen. That by his death—the investment of himself—he has endowed us with the capacity to be reconcilers. Through our relationships we are instruments of peace and forgiveness.

We become reflectors of healing to one another. And we learn that our identity—though no longer up for grabs through the playing out of some role (parent, child, lover, spouse, friend)—is essentially communal. It is affirmed, confirmed and reflected back to us by those in whom we invest.

There's good news and bad news to such an arrangement. First the bad news. One, we can no longer pretend that we're self-sufficient. Because we are not. There will always be the temptation to overestimate our will-power, our self-control and our stamina. In so doing, we too easily burn our bridges of support and balance. And if we're not careful, we can see this book as another opportunity to collect the necessary data to continue our solo flight to happiness. We miss the point that the thrust of the book forces us to see how much more we need each other on the road to intimate relations.

Two, we are sometimes connected to persons who are not necessarily pleasant to be connected with. Some of our relationships—family of origin, church family, anonymous support groups, etc.—cannot be readily dismissed in favor of some anticipated better relationships in the future. The issue is not easily resolved anticipating how our capacity to experience intimacy will increase after the "right people" enter our lives. We see, in fact, that our current relationships may be the necessary soil to work through the significant issues (trust, boundaries, respect, anger, expectations) we face.

Now the good news.

We don't need to pretend that we have got our act together. There's no need to live as if there's something to prove, or someone to impress, or points to earn. If our ego is already intact in the hands of a faithful God, community becomes a gift, not another battleground for self-worth. In community, we can begin to take the first step—to live and choose and respond—as if we are tough enough to be soft.

A lifestyle of intimacy (being human, open, real) is our pursuit and our task. That we understand. But being connected as the necessary price to pay? Now there's the rub!

And yet (I'm sure the objection will be raised) didn't we

conclude our last chapter with a summons to solitude—through the regular practice of sabbath? Isn't this a contradiction? By a summons to solitude aren't we advocating isolation?

This answer is no. We get confused, however, if we see this (community versus solitude) as an either-or dilemma, somehow to be resolved by choosing one option at the exclusion of the other. Such is not the case. But let's look back to help us clarify. The book is built on a premise that intimacy issues are foundationally identity issues. In other words, we cannot be victims of intimacy. We come to intimate behaviors by way of ownership—taking responsibility—for the choices we make: the boundaries we erect, the antenna we send up, and the responses we make.

We are—by nature—response-able. Creatures able to take responsibility. Able to make investments. Able to stand by commitments. Such a reality assumes that there are also those to whom we respond. Those to whom we commit. In other words, we are not inanimate objects. We are human. And our ability to make choices and take responsibility is illumined in the face of the other (the friend, the lover, the spouse)—the one to whom we respond. It is precisely when we are connected—response-able—that we are most human. It is as if the coin of our identity has two sides. One is our perception of our self in solitude. The other is the perception of our self via the community. The perception of our identity mirrored back to us in relationships where we are response-able.

In addition, we made it clear that we are able to make healthy choices in such relationships when we know that our identity is intact—no longer up for grabs via performance and accumulation. To hear that reality, we must practice removing ourselves (it's a choice) from preoccupations, worry and distractions which distort our identity. Hence, the practice of sabbath. The purpose of our solitude is not, then, for further self-consciousness—a continued strip-mining of the ego—which only encourages further isolation. The purpose of our solitude is self-awareness, and the permission to embrace the continued revelation that we are loved by a relentless and tender Creator. Rather than leading to isolation, such an experience points more acutely to an awareness of our powerlessness, and our ongoing need for others. Solitude always sends us back to community.

To help us further understand this ingredient, let's look at it through the lens of community, friendship, and liturgy.

The Necessity of Community

Alcoholics don't need more lectures on the evil of drink. They need Alcoholics Anonymous. In the same way, we don't need more lectures on intimacy. We need a support structure. A community. A place where everyone knows our name. A place where we invest ourselves. A place where we can make commitments. A place where we can be response-able. A place to practice the aerobics of intimacy.

This is all the more important in that we recognize our urge will always be toward isolation. We have been inculcated with the spirit of a nation that worships at the alter of the self. We are a culture that opts for information via sermons, motivation via self-help books, inspiration via entertainment, and affirmation and self worth via year-end reports and bottom-line proformas. It has left us spiritually and relationally malnourished.

Individualism lies at the very core of American culture. In fact, argue the authors of the book *Habits of the Heart,* it has been given ontological reverence. So much so, that we believe that "anything that would violate our right to think for ourselves, judge for ourselves, make our own decisions, live our lives as we see fit, is not only morally wrong, it is sacrilegious" (*Habits,* p. 142). We were raised with a cultural perception of development that taught us maturity is to be achieved in complete autonomy. The purpose—from the cradle to the grave—is to slowly delete (or grow beyond) people who keep us dependent. Blatantly popularized in a remark by a popular novelist, who said, "The only way to live happily in Hollywood is not to need anything from anyone."

Here again, we suffer from an either-or dilemma. In our Western mind set, dependence is viewed as a weakness, as equivalent to "childlike" (implying childish or needy), and therefore an enemy to be avoided. We would benefit from the Zen perspective which sees childbirth as the moment of isolation, and our journey to maturity as a movement from isolation to interdependence in old age. What's at stake is not that we relinquish our identity, or become externally referenced, or dependent for our self-worth, but that our humanness depends on (or reveals itself by) our being connected. Our humanity—our capacity to be vulnerable, giving, receiving, loving, trusting—blossoms in the soil of connectedness. For to be connected means that we are less tempted to overestimate our will power, or our reservoir of self-control, or our capacity for finding meaning through interiority.

At some point, we must accept the fact that we are all incomplete people in a broken world, and none of us can make it alone. The price tag here is our daily acknowledgment that we are not fragmented units. That after all is said and done, we go from here as fellow strugglers on the way.

That is why we need each other. And that is why God gave us the Church. Because none of us is complete in isolation. Granted, the Church doesn't necessarily have a very good track record for providing healthy models of nurturing communities. In fact, in many instances the outcome is blatantly destructive. But that does not nullify the need or the reality of the Church's purpose. We all need a place where we can join a community of memory joggers. Why? Because we have lousy memories about who and what really owns us. Because we have forgotten that our identity (both the dark side and the light) is intact in the hands of a faithful God, and we have no more need of continually repeating self-destructive behaviors, or proving our worth by accumulating points on the self-discipline scale of 1 to 10, or by handing our identity over to another—by being manager or rescuer or martyr—for approval and reassurance. Because we need others to "listen to us, to learn from, to go to for help, to talk to, to take care of, to love and to be loved by. Our personality is formed, grows, and develops through our interaction with others. They heal us, protect us, challenge us, comfort us" (Greeley, *The Great Mysteries,* p. 94). In community we are reminded that we are more than just the sum of our parts.

Isolation is the killer. And there is no benefit in pretending that we are the solitary hero—fighting all odds and standing alone. More than ever, we need to join with fellow journeyers and strugglers—for perspective, and support, and accountability. We do a disservice to ourselves—and to the discussion—by assuming that we can approach the subject as isolated units. As if intimacy is possible in a vacuum. Coupled with an erroneous assumption that intimacy is strictly behavioral, then, we come to the decision-making process with the hope that it is primarily a left-brain activity, where sufficient knowledge or information will resolve any dilemma. The emphasis is on the cognitive, where black and white, right and wrong, and correct answers are more important than health.

In the church, we have fanned the flames of this rugged individualism by advocating a "just me and Jesus" theology. The result is unfortunate. Striving to prove our worthiness as individual players, we see vulnerability as a threat, and work to strengthen our self-discipline, believing that we can handle it—whether it be the struggle of relational and sexual issues, addictive issues, or just life in general—on our own. But the fact that we are not above the struggle only causes us to repress our real feelings in favor of those which are more acceptable, still living life behind the mask of public opinion.

The bottom line is unavoidable. We cannot handle life on our own. We need friends. Granted, self-sufficiency is our preference. But we need friends. We may not have a good track record in this area. But we need friends. Friends—real friends—may be difficult to find. But we need friends. Because life was not meant to be handled on our own.

Some of us attempt to avoid that need by busily accumulating large numbers of friends. We create the illusion that we are open and vulnerable and relational, while in reality using the infrequency and superficiality of many relationships to hide—even from ourselves. Intimate with everyone, one author reminds us, we are intimate with no one.

Friendship as Sacrament

Friendship. It is a word easily bantered about, and either assumed or implied about most relationships. There is no shortage of material—books, tapes, movies and cards—on the subject of friendship. And my intention is not to introduce any additional new revelations about what it means to be a friend. Instead, we need to pause long enough to remove the word friend from the plethora of definitions that surround it. In such a sea of good-willed cultural diagnosis and commentary, we can too easily lose sight of the fact that friendship, before it is anything, is a sacrament.

Our minds conjure up images of an Irish pub at the turn of the century, where the "lads" have all gathered to tip a few stouts. The press of bodies, the laughter, and the smell of ale all mingle to create the backdrop for a gift. No sophisticated expertise here. It is a picture of a relaxed and permanent fellowship, very much at the core of their life.

Why is such a view of friendship important? Because in this world, we walk through the mine-fields of fear and mistrust. And we are surrounded by the rubble of broken relationships and communities.

In a Joseph Heller novel, Bob Slocum, the fictional narrator, encapsulates the nature of human relationships in a description of his workmates in a company where he has worked for almost twenty years. The theme, says Slocum, is fear.

"In my department, there are six people who are afraid of me, and one small secretary who is afraid of all of us. I have one other person working for me who is not afraid of anyone, not even me. . . . The thought occurs to me often that there must be mail clerks, office boys and girls, stock boys, messengers, and assistants of all kinds and ages who are afraid of everyone in the company" (Joseph Heller, *Something Happened,* p. 12).

It is a picture of a protective and anxious culture. We come to relationships guarded. Tired. Measured. It's a repeat of an earlier theme. We make hurtful choices not out of calculation or cruelty, but out of fear.

That is all the more reason why friendship is important. The glimmer of hope in a darkened world. And that is all the more reason to see friendship as a sacrament. A sacrament is a physical sign (or manifestation) of a non-physical reality—in this case, a sign of grace. It is a sign of hope in a world where we believe our relational dilemmas can be resolved via technique and insight and will power. In short, friends cannot be bought or won. They are a gift. And as a gift—as a sacrament or gift of grace—they remind us of our fragile human nature and our need and permission to receive. For in receiving, friendships become the building blocks toward intimacy.

Community and Commitments

It means that it's inventory time for all of us. Don't worry, there's no quiz at the end of this book to ensure that everyone learned the right answers. Remember, intimacy is not a destination, but the journey.

On this journey, where do we go to get nurtured? Where do we go to get our memory jogged? Where are we responseable? Where will we go to digest this material? I suppose we could react to those questions with some guilt, chastising ourselves for withdrawing, feeling the pain of those days we've gone through rough times without friends, and wishing we were different in personality and capable of attracting companions and allies. But guilt is not the answer. For our intention here is not to keep score, and our guilt can often be a way to keep us stuck and a way to avoid taking responsibility and moving on.

Such an inventory is not easy, given our sacred foundation of individual rights, and our ability to easily hide behind our multiple friendships, and communities which can easily take the form of a "lifestyle enclave." A community that becomes nothing more than a gathering of individuals who share common interests, hobbies and pursuits. In such a context, we are response-able only where our own needs are met. Church can easily become such a place of withdrawal. In a candid observation, Dietrich Bonhoeffer reminds us that, "The Christian community is not a spiritual sanatorium" (Bonhoeffer, p. 76).

It is a warning we must heed. For "community is not a collection of self-seeking individuals, not a temporary remedy, like Parents Without Partners, that can be abandoned as soon as a partner has been found, but a context within which personal identity is formed, a place where fluent self-awareness follows the currents of communal conversation and contributes to them" (*Habits of the Heart,* p. 135). In other words, community and friendship, by their very nature imply responsibility and commitment. Alone we have a tremendous capacity to lose that perspective. While we are alone, we believe in our ability to be self-sufficient and in our capacity to be able to love everyone. In community, we recognize that we are not capable to make life a solo flight, and can all too often be unmerciful and inhuman. Community moves love to the realm of maturity—where it is binding, treacherous, full of responsibility and physicality. The love of dreams must be given up for the love of real life.

What are the elements of this responsibility called community?

1) *The necessity of confession.*

There can be no lone rangers in community. And like the monk from our earlier illustration, we are not condemned to fight our battles alone. This is a difficult concept to embrace when we continue to believe that vulnerability is a weakness, unable to see the freedom that comes from a lifestyle of vulnerability through confession.

Confession (coming out of hiding) has been a theme throughout the entire book. It is, we said, the first step on any journey. Confession is a place to own our dandelions. Our fear. Our neediness. Our self-destructive bent. Our addictions. And our internal clutter. Confession looks at the demons within and acknowledges that victory will never come through repression or will power. Confession lets the demons out, and learns to tame them. Confession lets us live without needing to pretend we are something we are not. Confession moves us out from under the tyranny of the compulsion to be self-sufficient.

That's why I recommend support groups—as communities of confession. They can play a very important role in our relational and personal healing and growth, by providing an environment for ongoing confession and encouragement toward personal responsibility. Support groups are intentional gatherings of three to twelve (though some go as high as twenty or thirty) that meet regularly (at least twice a month) committed to the purpose of nurturing and encouraging each other in specific areas of personal, spiritual and mutual growth. Support groups, then, are not just serendipitous gatherings. They are intentional. The purpose of the group is focus, affirmation and accountability. Groups vary according to their focus. Some groups are intense in their commitments and by their very nature long term. Some are more loosely structured (like most anonymous groups), and are there when you need them. Some groups are more directive (like therapy groups, or discussion-oriented groups), and some tend to be caring groups with no predetermined agenda.

Our culture, with its emphasis upon individualism, sees support groups as optional behavior at best. Though we are beginning to see the value of support groups, it's not uncommon to hear the inevitable, "but aren't they primarily for people with problems?"

It is not our intention to add support groups to the already long list of mandated behaviors, as if a group is another obligation necessary for our acceptance. On the other hand, I would be remiss if I didn't point to the danger of continued isolation. There is no magic wand in a support group. But support groups (twelve step groups, home support groups, church covenant groups) can be necessary reminders to us of our identity—a place where we don't need to perform, nor do we need to give in to the equal tyranny of our selfishness. It is a place where we don't run from ambiguity. Where we do not need to squelch doubt. Or run from pain or the shadow side. Where we can celebrate healthy choices. And where we can be a place of healing for the wounds that come from unhealthy choices. It can be a channel where God's grace can become real.

2) *The place of mentoring.*

Mentoring is the choice to align myself with people who will not demand too little of me. Throughout church history, this process has been called spiritual direction. And because of the somewhat formidable sound of that title, it is sometimes called spiritual friendship.

Why do we need spiritual direction? Or a spiritual friend? Because in isolation we are prone to short-sightedness, self-righteousness, and bigotry. We may see only a part instead of the whole. Because we are all in need of a memory jogger, who helps remind us of our real strengths and weaknesses. One who helps remind us that we are not expendable, nor are we irreplaceable. A spiritual director (or spiritual friend) is one who helps validate and reinforce the journey—one who validates the voice of God in me.

Who can be a spiritual director? Someone who has been on the path a bit longer than I have. A spiritual friend is a fellow traveler who is God centered, confident, and yet human, a fellow struggler who has experienced failures, temptations and pitfalls. Through their own journey they help point us to God.

3) *The role of accountability.*

With the public erosion of morality in recent years, the subject of accountability has received much press. It's essential, we are told. And yet, there is some continued difficulty in clearly defining what is meant by the word accountability. Too often, we elicit its aid in defense of our paranoia. It becomes a protective wall to maintain a visible us versus them delineation. It is a term needed to distinguish the white hats from the black hats.

Accountability, however, must be more than just a means to protect orthodoxy. Viewed in a relational context, the message of accountability is more than saying "No" to commandment violators. Accountability is an extension of community, and is therefore built on relationships. In the context of a relationship—of connectedness—it is the permission to say "Yes" to responsibility. Yes to investment. Yes to healthy boundaries. Accountability is a relational protection for my bent toward unhealthy and isolating choices.

Communities of Memory: The Role of Liturgy

Where do we go from here? I realize that there's a tendency for us to run off newly armed with a collection of data and theories, infused with a sense of hope about some insight that will breathe new life into our relationships.

It's here that we need to be reminded that this journey toward intimacy is an aerobic activity. It is not resolved or completed or settled with correct information. It is a journey of practice and time, of trial and error, of choices and commitments, of risk and pain. And the truth is that we will all mess up sooner than we want to, and make mistakes more often than we had expected. That's why community is essential. For in community our identity memory can be jogged. We need such a place, where memory jogging is a rehearsal of affirmation and encouragement and the call to health. Memory jogging, then, is the role of liturgy, or story telling.

There is a delightful Hasidic tale about the power of stories—the liturgy of memory jogging. Whenever the people of the great Rabbi Israel Baal Shem Tov were in great danger, the good rabbi would go to a particular place in the forest to meditate. There he would light a fire and say a special prayer. Whenever he did this, a miracle would happen and his people would be saved.

A generation later, when the people of his disciple, Magid of Mezritch, were faced with a crisis, Magid would emulate his master. But he had forgotten how to light a fire. So he would just go to the same spot in the forest and say the prayer his master had taught him. And God would perform a miracle for his people.

Another generation later, the people of the Rabbi Moshe-Leib of Sasov were faced with a crisis. The rabbi did not know how to light the fire, and he had forgotten the prayer. All he could remember was the place in the forest. So he simply went to the place and, as he had hoped, God delivered his people from danger.

The rabbi of the next generation, Israel of Rizhyn, did not know how to light the fire, did not know the prayer, and had no idea where the place in the forest was. But when his people were in great danger, he would sit in his armchair and tell the story of what had happened to his ancestors. And that was sufficient to save his people. (Rabbi Abraham Heschel, anecdote quoted by Ben Patterson, *The Grand Essentials,* p. 102.)

The community of memory—through story telling history as liturgy—becomes a community of hope. A place where our identity rises above the individual moments of culturally defined success or failure. A reminder that our identity is not just a matter of what we've done or failed to do, but to whom we belong.

There's a corollary story about two of my friends, Frog and Toad, introduced to us in a series by Arnold Lobel. Toad is sad because the mail hasn't come. And in fact, he has never received any mail, so mail time is always his sad time of day. To be a good friend, Frog sits with Toad awhile so that they can feel sad together. But Frog gets an idea and leaves quickly. With paper and pencil, Frog writes a letter to Toad. He gives it to a snail for delivery, and goes back to join his friend Toad. By this time, Toad is in bed, still discouraged over no mail, and no amount of encouragement by Frog can get him up to wait for the mail some more. Finally Frog tells Toad he wrote him a letter. "What'd you write in the letter?" Toad wanted to know. "I wrote, 'Dear Toad, I'm glad you're my best friend. Your best friend, Frog.'" said Frog. "Oh," said Toad, "That makes a very good letter." And Frog and Toad sat on the front porch to wait for the mail, feeling happy together.

Frog's letter to Toad is the stuff of liturgy. A sign of hope. It becomes a symbol, a story, a memory jogger for the ongoing outworking of their relationship. It is an offering of history, with an affirmation of, and an encouragement toward continued commitment and responsibility. And in a world of brokenness, it become a necessary foundation for the journey toward intimacy.

There's a humorous story about the general who said to the lieutenant, "Give me a report on where the enemy is." "Yes sir!" was the response. An hour later, the lieutenant returned with his report. "The enemy is to the north of us sir. The enemy is to the south of us sir. The enemy is to the east of us sir. The enemy is to the west of us sir. That's good news sir!"

"Good news, lieutenant?"

"Yes, sir. They can't get away from us now!"

Perhaps there's wisdom in that silly, simple response. For the fact is clear that all of us come to the subject of intimacy with enemies. We have enemies to the north of us—choices we've made in life which we wish we hadn't made, and no amount of replay on the memory video seems to make a difference. We have enemies to the south of us—choices and behaviors done against us that were unfair, hurtful and wrong, and we wonder why. We have enemies to the east of us—our lingering sense of insecurity, wondering if we'll ever have enough math whiz cards to be okay. And we have enemies to the west of us—a sense of fear and an ongoing commitment to build a wall of security and protection in an insecure world.

We may be hoping that someone—through a book or lecture or piece of advice—will take the enemies away, or overwhelm them, or prove that they are only illusions. We can't do that here. Nor was it ever our intention. We can only offer a promise: "Greater is the One who is in you than the enemies that surround you." And a warning: It is a promise impossible to hear in isolation.

Relationships are not easy . . . which is precisely why we need each other on the road ahead.

Epilogue

I hope you smiled. Laughed. Felt sadness. Even anger and some relief. And I hope you stopped—to listen, to celebrate, to enjoy. Above all else, I hope that you felt glad to be alive.

All books on relationships face the same obstacle. There will always be the temptation to give in to the lure of magic. We want answers! We want our problems solved! We want to arrive!

But life is not fair. Nor is it easily reducible to a handout on human relations. And to add to the frustration, no matter how enlightened we feel, relationships are tricky at best, and most of us know that we are not nearly as far along as we had wished. We are susceptible to a notion that there will be an award banquet at the end of this journey to honor those who traveled the farthest or the fastest. It is an infectious mentality that "glamorizes the power of the will" (Cermak, p. 121), overemphasizing the human potential and the power of positive thinking.

This journey, however, is not about perfection. Nor performance for that matter. Our perspective needs to be balanced with an understanding that life does not need to be overcome. The goal of our journey is integrity, played out in the small steps we take with everyday choices of investment and commitment.

Where do we go from here? We take the next step. And with that step comes the permission to embrace our humanity. It is best captured in the wisdom of the Serenity Prayer:

> "God grant me the wisdom to accept the things I cannot change,
> Strength to change the things I can,
> And wisdom to know the difference."

To walk the journey toward intimacy is to walk the journey toward being fully alive. It is not an easy path. And it will cost us our comfort and our illusions. It is a price very few have the courage or the willingness to pay. Because "one has to abandon altogether the search for security, and reach out to the risk of living with both arms. One has to embrace the world like a lover. One has to accept pain as a condition of existence. One has to court doubt and darkness as the cost of knowing. One needs a will stubborn in conflict, but apt always to total acceptance of every consequence of living and dying" (Morris West, *Shoes of the Fisherman,* p. 186).

Easy? No. Worth it? You bet.

For the secret is not fending life off, but learning to invite it in. And regardless of where you've been, or how far you think you have traveled, or have yet to travel, or how limited you think your resources are, or how much you think you've lost in the past, the journey always begins with today. Welcome to the journey!

Bibliography

Robert N. Bellah, *Habits of the Heart* (Berkeley: University of California Press, 1985).

Dietrich Bonhoeffer, *Ethics* (New York: Macmillan, 1955).

John Bradshaw, *Healing the Shame That Binds You* (Deerfield Beach: HCI, 1988).

Frederick Buechner, *Telling the Truth* (San Francisco: Harper and Row, 1977).

———. *Wishful Thinking* (San Francisco: Harper and Row, 1973).

———. *Now and Then* (San Francisco: Harper and Row, 1983).

Robert Capon, *Between Noon and Three* (San Francisco: Harper and Row, 1982).

———. *The Parables of the Kingdom* (Grand Rapids: Zondervan, 1985).

Patrick Carnes, *Out of the Shadows (The Sexual Addiction)* (Minneapolis: Comp Care, 1983).

Timmon Cermak, *A Time to Heal* (Los Angeles: Tarcher, 1988).

Keith Clark, *An Experience of Celibacy* (Notre Dame: Ave Maria Press, 1982).

———. *Being Sexual . . . and Celibate* (Notre Dame: Ave Maria Press, 1986).

———. *Make Space, Make Symbols* (Notre Dame: Ave Maria Press, 1974).

Anthony de Mello, *The Song of the Bird* (New York: Image Books, 1984).

James Dittes, *The Male Predicament* (San Francisco: Harper and Row, 1985).

Merle A. Fossum and Marilyn J. Mason, *Facing Shame* (New York: Norton, 1986).

Victor Frankl, *Man's Search for Meaning* (New York: Pocket Books, 1963).

———. *The Unheard Cry for Meaning* (New York: Touchstone, 1978).

Donald Goergen, *The Sexual Celibate* (New York: Image, 1979).

Andrew Greeley, *Sexual Intimacy* (London: W.H. Allen, 1973).

———. *The Great Mysteries* (San Francisco: Harper and Row, 1976).

Tim Hansel, *You Gotta Keep Dancin'* (Elgin, IL: David C. Cook, 1985).

David Hassel, *Dark Intimacy* (Mahwah, NJ: Paulist Press, 1986).

Joseph Heller, *Something Happened* (New York: Alfred A. Knopf, 1974).

Terry Hershey, *Beginning Again* (Nashville: Thomas Nelson, 1986).

———. *Intimacy: The Longing of Every Human Heart* (Salem: Harvest House, 1987).

Robert Johnson, *We* (San Francisco: Harper and Row, 1983).

Sam Keen, *The Passionate Life* (San Francisco: Harper and Row, 1983).

Morton and Barbara Kelsey, *Sacrament of Sexuality* (Warwick, NY: Amity House, 1986).

Eugene Kennedy, *The Trouble with Being Human* (New York: Image Books, 1986).

Harold Kushner, *When All You've Ever Wanted Isn't Enough* (New York: Summit, 1986).

William Lenters, *The Freedom We Crave* (Grand Rapids: Wm. B. Eerdmans, 1985).

George Leonard, *The End of Sex* (Los Angeles: Tarcher, 1983).

C. S. Lewis, *Mere Christianity* (New York: Macmillan, 1943).

———. *God in the Dock* (Grand Rapids: Wm. B. Eerdmans, 1970).

———. *Christian Reflections* (Grand Rapids: Wm. B. Eerdmans, 1967).

Susan Littwin, *The Postponed Generation* (New York: Morrow, 1986).

Gordon MacDonald, *Ordering Your Private World* (Nashville: Thomas Nelson, 1984).

Alan Loy McGinnis, *The Friendship Factor* (Minneapolis: Augsburg, 1979).

Thomas P. Malone and Patrick T. Malone, *The Art of Intimacy* (New York: Prentice Hall, 1987).

Thomas Merton, *Raids on the Unspeakable* (New York: New Directions, 1960).

Alice Miller, *The Drama of the Gifted Child* (New York: Basic Books, 1981).

———. *Thou Shalt Not Be Aware* (New York: Meridian, 1986).

Keith and Andrea Miller, *The Single Experience* (Waco: Word, 1981).

Keith Miller, *Sin: the Ultimate Addiction* (San Francisco: Harper and Row, 1987).

Susan Muto, *Celebrating the Single Life* (New York: Doubleday, 1982).

Donald Nicholl, *Holiness* (New York: Seabury, 1981).

Ben Patterson, *The Grand Essentials* (Waco: Word, 1987).

Scott Peck, *The Road Less Traveled* (New York: Touchstone, 1978).

Walter Perry, *The Thanatos Syndrome* (New York: Farrar, Straus, and Giroux, 1987).

Laurel Richardson, *New Other Woman* (New York: The Free Press, 1985).

Philip Roth, *The Professor of Desire* (New York: Farrar, Straus, and Giroux, 1977).

May Sarton, *Journal of a Solitude* (New York: Norton, 1973).

Anne Wilson Schaef, *Co-Dependence* (San Francisco: Harper and Row, 1986).

———. *Escape from Intimacy* (San Francisco: Haper and Row, 1989).

Merle Shain, *Some Men Are More Perfect Than Others* (New York: Bantam, 1973).

———. *When Lovers are Friends* (New York: Bantam, 1978).

Lewis Smedes, *Sex for Christians* (Grand Rapids: Wm. B. Eerdmans, 1976).

———. *Choices* (San Francisco: Harper and Row, 1986).
———. *Mere Morality* (Grand Rapids: Wm. B. Eerdmans, 1983).

Anthony Storr, *Solitude: A Return to the Self* (New York: Free Press, 1988).

Gerald Vann, *Moral Dilemmas* (New York: Simon and Schuster, 1986).

Judith Viorst, *Necessary Losses* (New York: Simon and Schuster, 1986).

Morris West, *Shoes of the Fisherman* (New York: Penguin Books, 1974).